Praise for
*Staying Alive in the Funeral
and Cemetery Profession*

"When you need surgery, you go to an expert surgeon; when you need an expert in the funeral industry, you go to Johnson Consulting Group. Whether you're buying, selling, or growing your business, Jake's experience and wisdom will help you achieve optimal outcomes from your investment and efforts!"

—Sheldon Harris, Partner, CEO Coaching International

"Jake and his team of experienced professionals are a valuable resource to all areas of the funeral profession. This book is just a sample of their deep insights."

—Mike Webb, CEO, Service Corporation International

"Jake Johnson has written a book that, as I read it, seemed like my thirty-three-year career condensed into just a few pages! I have experienced and lived nearly every single topic in Jake's book, but most of it I learned the hard way, through trial and error. This book is a must-read for any funeral professional in any stage of their career! For some it will help them exit successfully, and for others it will help them build successful businesses and grow them wisely. I feel like I lived my career over again by reading this book and wished I would have had it available to me years ago! Two thumbs up, Jake!"

—Rick Allnutt, Former Owner, Allnutt Family Companies

"Jake has touched on many valuable lessons and tools in this book, and I only wish I had read it twenty years ago. It is no secret the funeral industry has changed tremendously over the last thirty years and continues to do so, with higher cremation rates, new competition, and declining revenue per call, not to mention the ever-increasing costs of doing business. Over the years of working with Jake and Johnson Consulting Group, our business operated stronger and was more financially stable. Our surveys and performance improved. All the while, having 'real-time' financials and sales analysis from the accounting team kept the train on track and rolling right ahead. Then when the time came to sell our business, once again I turned to Jake and his team. Their metrics for valuations and recommendations were spot on, which ultimately lead to an easy decision for the business and my family.

"This book can be an invaluable tool to the owner trying to be more relevant, a new generation coming into the business, or a family thinking about succession planning for the future. Jake and the team of experts at JCG will work with you to create a plan today and help you navigate the future in funeral service successfully and profitably. Your business and personal life will be better for it."

—Laurens Fish III, Former Owner, Weed Corley Fish Funeral Homes

"Jake Johnson offers fresh perspective and a progressive take on the current state of the death care industry. His years of experience in all aspects of funeral service make this book a must-read for anyone interested in acquisitions or taking their existing business to the next level."

—Kenny Knauss, Past President, Palm Mortuaries and Cemeteries

"Jake and the Johnson Consulting team have helped hundreds of funeral and cemetery owners. As a result they have a wonderful view of our profession—where we've been, where we're headed, and some great thinking on how to best get there."

—Jay Waring, COO, Service Corporation International

"In a profession that is experiencing so much consumer change and disruption, Jake's message is the most relevant guide to future growth and success available today!"

—Walker Posey, Owner, Posey Funeral Directors

"The content of this book proves that you can grow your business successfully—despite rising cremation rates—through innovation and recruiting the right team. Embracing these changes will help you leap forward. This book has reaffirmed to me that the funeral industry is constantly evolving and how to strategize for the future. Jake's wisdom is certainly a refreshing yet forward-thinking outlook on future profitability, innovation, and collaboration as keys to success in our industry. This is certainly a great read for all funeral and cemetery professionals."

—Paul C. St. Pierre, Sixth-Generation Funeral Director

"I often am skeptical when I see a must-read for our profession, but this is a must-read. Jake delivers beyond words an excellent summation of what business owners must navigate and consider. His wisdom from real-life experience is more than advice; it is a true testimonial of someone who cares deeply for our profession."

—James H. Busch, President, Busch Funeral and
Crematory Services, Cleveland, Ohio

"Jake Johnson has written an excellent book that very accurately identifies the current challenges and opportunities for improvement in modern death care businesses. His creativity in the manner that he presents his information is matched by his unique and very deep knowledge of funeral service operations. There are few funeral professionals who have witnessed firsthand all aspects of funeral home and cemetery management as Jake. His vast and varied experiences are unique among peers, and this book offers a recipe for best practices and improvement in business operations for a multifaceted profession in challenging and changing times."

—Charles M. Billow, Billow Funeral Homes & Crematory

"I started Johnson Consulting some twenty years ago and turned it over to Jake's capable hands shortly thereafter with great success. Now the book … great information based on many years of experience. A must-read!"

—Tom Johnson, Founder, Johnson Consulting Group

"Jake Johnson is truly a 'unicorn extraordinaire' who possesses a deep and vast knowledge of the funeral and cemetery business. Jake earned his stripes and credibility by demonstrating how, when, and what an owner should do to grow revenue, reduce cost, or position themselves for a sale."

—Steve Tidwell, Senior Vice President, Sales and Marketing, Service Corporation International

"Having been a client of JCG for more than ten years, I credit Jake and his firm for providing invaluable tools that have allowed our funeral homes, cemeteries, crematory, and flower shops to grow via the JCG accounting and management reporting they provide. *Staying Alive in the Funeral and Cemetery Profession* by Jake Johnson is a must-read. Jake walks through the strategic steps owners *must* do to maximize the value of their enterprises."

—W. Warren Claybar, President, Claybar Funeral Homes and Hillcrest Memorial Gardens

Staying Alive *in the*

Funeral and Cemetery Profession

Staying Alive in the Funeral and Cemetery Profession

Building a Business, Weathering Changes, and Finding Growth

Jake Johnson

Published by Advantage, Charleston, South Carolina.
Member of Advantage Media Group.

ADVANTAGE is a registered trademark, and the Advantage colophon is a trademark of Advantage Media Group, Inc.

Printed in the United States of America.

10 9 8 7 6 5 4 3 2 1

ISBN: 978-1-64225-089-3
LCCN: 2019914683

Book design by Matthew Morse.

This publication is designed to provide accurate and authoritative information in regard to the subject matter covered. It is sold with the understanding that the publisher is not engaged in rendering legal, accounting, or other professional services. If legal advice or other expert assistance is required, the services of a competent professional person should be sought.

Advantage Media Group is proud to be a part of the Tree Neutral® program. Tree Neutral offsets the number of trees consumed in the production and printing of this book by taking proactive steps such as planting trees in direct proportion to the number of trees used to print books. To learn more about Tree Neutral, please visit **www.treeneutral.com**.

Advantage Media Group is a publisher of business, self-improvement, and professional development books and online learning. We help entrepreneurs, business leaders, and professionals share their Stories, Passion, and Knowledge to help others Learn & Grow. Do you have a manuscript or book idea that you would like us to consider for publishing? Please visit **advantagefamily.com** or call **1.866.775.1696**.

I would like to dedicate this book to you! Thank you for taking an interest in this profession and making it the best you can!

CONTENTS

About the Author

Jake Johnson has rapidly advanced into senior leadership roles and gained respect throughout the funeral and cemetery industries. He is known as an innovator, change agent, and thought leader. Jake's success is based on his unique ability to identify simple solutions for complex business problems and communicate across all levels of the organization, instilling positive morale, empowerment, and employee ownership to drive service excellence. His strong foundation in accounting, financial analysis, and EBITDA forecasting is complemented by technology savvy and broad general management qualifications in business development and operations.

As president and CEO of Johnson Consulting, Jake provides strategic direction and marketing innovations that laid the groundwork for the company's rapid growth, gaining recognition as the premier total solutions provider within the funeral industry. In his former position as executive vice president and general manager at Palm Mortuaries and Cemeteries, he provided key operations leadership to the Palm Cemetery Division. During his time at Palm Mortuaries, he handled funeral arrangements and funeral directing, and he was a funeral home manager for a seven-hundred-plus annual funeral call location. Jake began his career at Keystone Group

Holdings (now Dignity Memorial Network) as associate director, corporate development, where his financial analysis and forecasting expertise was foundational to the firm's growth. Jake's educational credentials include a BSBA degree in management with an emphasis in accounting and financial analysis from Xavier University in Cincinnati, Ohio. Rounding out his financial portfolio, he is an Arizona-licensed real estate agent and licensed investment advisor representative. Jake is also a member emeritus of the Funeral Service Foundation Board.

Acknowledgments

I want to thank my father for his leadership and professional advice over the years. I want to thank Steve Tidwell for his mentorship, and for believing in me when I was starting my career. I thank Kenny Knauss for allowing me the opportunity to work in the business, for his great organization, and for showing the ability of even the busiest of people to return a call or email right away! I would like to thank Mike Webb and Jay Waring for their friendship and for showing me just how successful one can be in this space with hard work. I'd also like to thank Rubin Lariz, who showed me that, no matter hard you work, there are always things to be done. And most importantly I want to thank my wife, Robyn, and my two boys, Logan and Carson, for supporting my long hours and time away so that I may create the most success I can in this profession!

Preface

This book aims to help people in our profession recognize how change impacts their business in more ways than meet the eye, such as how decisions impact enterprise value. I want the reader to consider carefully how they spend their day to get the most out of the value they bring and to put the lesser-value tasks out to others; to discover that there are opportunities in this business now and in the future if you go after them with all your efforts; and to know that, as they say, "There is always somebody out there that is bigger, better, stronger." My aim for the reader is to *be* that somebody! It is up to you. There is no wrong answer, but that also means there should be no excuse on your part. You can either make it happen or wonder what happened. It's your choice.

Foreword

Jake Johnson's *Staying Alive in the Funeral and Cemetery Profession* is refreshing, visionary, challenging, and insightful—with a good touch of subtle dry humor! Truly, it is invigorating, expansive, and exciting to read.

Jake's background in funeral service and cemeteries is remarkable and unique. Except for embalming, Jake has literally done it all and at every level. Significantly, his early career formation and experience was outside of the "family business" of Jake's iconic and highly successful father, Tom Johnson, truly one of the most distinguished in the history of our industry. After, Jake had very extensive upward success in his career, and then Jake joined Johnson Consulting in its early days, and after many years of being a major contributor in the success and growth of JCG, he became his father, Tom's, successor and serves today as its CEO. Since Jake became the executive leader at JCG, the firm has grown exponentially as a full-service consulting firm—offering its clients every innovative service imaginable to best serve them at their very difficult times and offering its client owners and their associates the opportunity to enjoy a successful enterprise—a true win-win for all!

On a personal level, my respect, friendship, and gratitude to Jake; Tom, the founder; and the JCG team is profound. I have often said and continue to say, "The single best business decision I have ever made was engaging Johnson Consulting nearly a decade ago!" Our relationship with Jake and the team has allowed us to grow significantly and challenged our associates, leadership team, and me to become far better across *every* metric. It has been fun, added to our passion, and been a great return on investment, and with positive expectancy for the future, we will continue this great and wonderful relationship!

Death, taxes, and *change* are the only guarantees of life! "Caring for the dead while serving the living" has been and, in some form, will always be a part of societies and civilizations. *How* we change and adapt (or not) will determine our role in this honorable service to others. Jake Johnson's insight is the "cutting edge" of maximizing our today while preparing for our new and different tomorrow—all while having passionate enjoyment in the process!

Whether you are young and considering entering our profession, early in your career journey, midstage, a serious (or potential) investor, or just a "classic citizen" like me (I prefer this term to "old"!), *Staying Alive in the Funeral and Cemetery Profession* is a must-read, in my opinion. I am so very confident you will enjoy reading and inwardly digesting Jake's remarkable book, and you will be very happy you did so!

—Bill Hawkins
Founder, President
Angeleno Mortuaries Inc.

Introduction

You've worked diligently your whole life to build a successful funeral or cemetery business. Yet in the past few years—despite all your efforts—it can seem like a struggle. With so much effort and so little to show for it, you're feeling, well, like the walking dead.

You're not alone. The rise in cremation rates, ever-changing buying habits of today's consumers, and entrance of low-cost providers into the US market have delivered a blow to bottom lines. Funeral and cemetery professionals are working harder than ever for less. You have to wonder: Where is this all headed? And what kind of impact will it have on the value of your firm? After all, value is at the heart of what we do.

We all know that the perception of value changes along with customer preferences. And it can be a real challenge, considering that you're selling something no one wants to buy. But just how often do you weigh the impact of the business you bring in every day?

It can be said that the average funeral can provide up to $20,000 in enterprise value. So what happens when you don't serve a customer well? Serving one less family for the year may just cost the operation $20,000 in enterprise value. You could argue that these things happen, but the real question is, how can you ensure your business will thrive in the current economic climate rather than ... decline?

Many businesses struggle to answer questions like this one. With roughly 80 percent of funeral operations in small towns—averaging just three to seven employees each—it's hard to see the bigger picture and to know what's happening outside of your own organization. I've had the opportunity to do just that. I've occupied almost every role there is in the funeral and cemetery professions, from the grounds to the executive board. And as president and CEO of Johnson Consulting, the premier consulting firm for the funeral and cemetery professions across North America, I've bought, sold, and collaborated with thousands of businesses. I've seen firsthand the challenges they face and the factors that result in their success or failure—the good, the bad, and the ugly.

It may be less obvious today, in a world where social media seems to highlight just how green the grass is on the other side, but this is still a great business to be in. There are plenty of opportunities to refine, expand, or sell what is likely the most valuable asset you have. That's what we'll do here. The insights in this book—compiled over more than two decades of experience—can help you find more success, whatever your goals may be. But before we jump into the *how*, let me give you some of the *why*: my background.

I've been around the funeral business for as long as I can remember. I originate from Batesville, Indiana, home to the United States' largest casket manufacturer. If you were in Batesville—which has a population of about seven thousand people—you were most likely involved with the Batesville Casket Company in one way or another. My connection came through my father's side of the family, who knew the company's owners, the Hillenbrands, and eventually through my father himself.

Back in the day, when it was the norm to follow in your parents' footsteps, my dad thought he'd be a banker like his father, who was president of the local Batesville bank. That's not quite how things worked out, though. He had joined Fifth Third Bank in Cincinnati, Ohio, and was doing quite well. But banking was slower than my dad pictured. A serial entrepreneur and salesman by nature, he wanted more action. So he approached Batesville Casket Company to seek out employment in his hometown. After several interviews, he became the sales training manager for the company and found himself learning how to sell and merchandise caskets. The sales aspect of the job provided more excitement than banking offered, and Dad never turned back. He eventually implemented and ran the national accounts program for Batesville Casket, which negotiated contracts with larger firms in the United States. The rest of his career—and all of mine—would revolve around the funeral and cemetery professions.

My father's work took us to San Diego, California, where he was general manager of Greenwood Memorial Park, a very large cemetery/mortuary combination. When that company sold, it was on to Los Angeles, where he became president of Pierce Brothers Mortuaries and Cemeteries, then the largest funeral operation in Southern California. Pierce Brothers had fallen on tough times, and my dad was brought in to revive it. With him as my primary role model, when it came time for me to find summer work, a cemetery seemed like the most logical choice. The grounds at Pierce Brothers Valley Oaks in Westlake Village became my domain. I pulled weeds, cleared sidewalks, and trimmed rosebushes. It was a formative experience for me: the first place I ever got my hands dirty. It was also where I learned to drive, mostly because it was safe—there was no one I could hit that would die again. At the cemetery, I also had a manager who made a real difference in my life: Ruben Lariz. Ruben would always tell me my options: "*La pluma* or *la pala*"—the pen or the shovel. He worked me hard, with the goal of making sure that I would find my way from the grounds into an office. In many ways, my deep appreciation for the funeral and cemetery profession began there, on those grounds. It was humbling to see how hard the groundskeepers worked, and I promised myself that if I was ever in a position to manage a staff, I would treat them well and make sure my customers did the same.

Meanwhile, my father was working to turn the business around at Pierce Brothers. He was addressing the company workflow, consolidating where necessary, and holding roundtables with staff to figure out how to grow. Everyone left Dad alone because they knew that if they did, he would do his job as if he were the owner. And he was good at it. Pierce Brothers' owner at the time, self-made millionaire Joe Allbritton, had wanted to sell the business for $10 million before my dad came in. The highest offer had been $6 million. After Dad was done with it, a decade or so later, the company was worth well over $150 million. In fact, when Mr. Allbritton finally had a buyer—Service Corporation International, the world's largest chain of funeral homes and cemeteries—it was Dad he called to help him carry out the transition.

The sale was rough for my dad; he had invested so much time in the company. And so after it was through, he told himself that, going forward, he wouldn't be doing that kind of work for anyone but himself. He started his own acquisition company, Prime Succession, in Batesville, Indiana in 1992. I had just graduated high school, and I wasn't about to move from Los Angeles back to that sleepy town, so I began attending Santa Barbara City College. But without any family in California, I soon got lonely. It was through another funeral profession connection that I found Xavier University in Cincinnati, which is just forty-five minutes from Batesville. Michael Saint Pierre, who ran Wilson Funeral Homes in Indianapolis, had a son, Paul, who went to Xavier, and he showed me around. I graduated with a management degree, but I also took electives in subjects such as tax and financial statement analysis, things I knew I wanted to be part of my skill set.

My coursework at Xavier combined with a few traits I've had since birth would help shape my professional path. I've always been all about organization: if I was in the living room playing with my toys, they were lined up from big to small. Also, I thrive on my own, I never have a problem trying something new, and I try not to get stuck in analysis paralysis. If I can't find something I need or want, I'll invent it.

This mentality meant I didn't really need much direction; I liked to work, to fix things, to create them from scratch. And along with my accounting skills, I carried these tendencies into my first real job: working for my dad as an accountant. I was a little intimidated—my dad had around fifty employees, and no one in our family had ever considered working for his company—but I handled it as I should have. I walked on eggshells, and I didn't say crap if my mouth was full of it.

Soon after I joined Prime, the investor group that backed Dad decided to sell. The business went to Loewen Group, a big player in the space. This meant I—and many at the Prime home office—would be let go. But my dad had been good to his partners, Bob Horn, Bill Cutter, Berny Gaarsoe, and Steve Tidwell, and they were ready to set out on their own. With the money from the transaction, they started an acquisition company by the name of Keystone Group Holdings, based in Tampa, Florida. Steve and Bob brought on Steve Shaffer, who had been controller of Prime Succession, and a gentleman by the name of Jim Price, who ran the Pierce Brothers cemetery I worked at in high school. They agreed to bring me along too.

As an acquisition firm with VC backing, our charge was to go out and buy funeral businesses, and I had a chance to be involved from the very first deal. I quickly rose to director of business development within Keystone Group. Then, in 1999, the funeral and cemetery space went through an incredible change.

In prior years, the purchase price multiples that buyers would pay were based on historical performance, with offers coming in at five or six times earnings before interest, taxes, depreciation, and amortization (EBITDA). But the problem with acquisition analysis is that you can convince yourself of anything. There's nothing in front of you that says you can't do it except your own imagination. And now, acquisition companies were creating a pro forma in which purchasing companies would increase revenues by 3, 5, even 10 percent depending on where sales were compared to other funeral homes in the market, which created a higher cash flow.

In addition, competition in the acquisition space was getting so fierce that companies were paying very high multiples for businesses. Multiples kept creeping up—six and a quarter, six and a half, seven, and beyond. It was a double whammy of sorts: creating cash that didn't yet exist at these businesses, then paying more on top of that to secure the sale.

An owner would believe he was getting a purchase price multiple of seven times, but because the acquisition company had created such a high EBITDA, it appeared to investors that the buyer was only paying six times the value. As such, the investment community didn't have a fair method to compare one company to another using earnings per share.

This was especially challenging with the purchase of cemeteries. Let's consider receivables for a second. In our business there are at-need receivables and preneed receivables. Whether it's a funeral home or a cemetery, if it's an at-need receivable, it probably will come due and paid in less than forty-five days. For funeral homes, the preneed receivable could be five to seven years; however, depending on the state, typically a large balance of those funeral home preneed receivables will be due into an insurance product (there are exceptions, though, as with some states it can still be favorable to sell funeral home trust products). Now, typically with a cemetery, those preneed receivables over five to seven years are due in a trust or in cash, depending on whether it's merchandise, property, or a service (state rules dictating of course). Because of this, if revenues weren't being projected correctly, or if as a buyer you misinterpreted the financial statement, you were in jeopardy of vastly overpaying for cemeteries. And the numbers couldn't keep inflating forever.

Loewen Group, the company that had purchased my dad's firm, went bankrupt due in part by overpaying for acquisitions. Service Corporation International, which was publicly traded, dropped a whopping 94 percent between 1998 and 2000.[1]

During this crazy time, I decided I would go back and work inside a funeral home to get boots-on-the-ground experience. I got a job working for Palm Mortuaries and Cemeteries in Las Vegas, Nevada, which was then one of the largest privately owned funeral businesses west of the Mississippi, with sixty-five hundred funeral calls, twenty-four hundred cemetery interments, a monument company, and one of the largest flower shops in Las Vegas. There was no job description for me. Ken Knauss, the owner, trusted that I was a good worker and a quick learner. He hired me with the knowledge that I had been doing accounting and financial analysis previously, but he told me, "If you're really serious about working in a funeral home, this is what you're going to get. I hope you enjoy it." Instead of sitting behind a computer, I was driving coaches and limousines and delivering flowers. Eventually, I began directing funerals and doing funeral arrangements. My next role was running one of the company's funeral homes, which held about seven hundred funerals a year, compared to the US average of 110. I went on to oversee cemetery operations before serving on the company's executive board.

Meanwhile, Dad was in retirement, but people were constantly reaching out to him for guidance. He decided he should start charging to legitimize the work he was doing—and potentially slow the influx of requests. At the same time, he got a call from an investment group that was

---

1   Greer, Jim, "SCI Stock Price Hits New Low as Death Rate Keeps Declining." *Houston Business Journal.* August 6, 2000. https://www.bizjournals.com/houston/stories/2000/08/07/newscolumn2.html.

interested in buying his old business from Loewen Group. They wanted him to help split those funeral homes out and return them to the former owners or find new buyers for them. From there, Johnson Consulting Group was born.

In 2004, Dad felt he had enough steady business to bring me on. That year, I created the first official marketing package for Johnson Consulting and we did our first deal. My dad also decided to buy three funeral homes on his own: one back in Batesville and two in Phoenix. With their support, I decided to move the wife and kids to Phoenix, where my father and siblings had moved already, and that was where we would conduct business for Johnson Consulting. After about a year of working out of my house, I decided I needed an office. One of the funeral homes Dad owned had a small building next to it that was basically being held up by termites. With some work, that 1,100-square-foot building became our first location.

In 2007, we started doing accounting, business consulting, and customer surveys. By 2008, we had occupied all of the available space in our building and remodeled it as many times as we could—even turning the room that had once housed the hot water heater into an office. With no more room to expand, we bought our current building, then the building next to us and another one three doors down.

Today, Johnson Consulting provides "total solutions" for every aspect of the funeral and cemetery business life cycle. Throughout my career, and as we've grown, I've seen the changes this business has weathered, and I understand where it's headed. And though change can be scary, it also provides a world of opportunity if you know how to harness it. That applies to anyone in funeral operations—managers, arrangers, directors, embalmers, and administrative support staff. Every role matters, and as such, everyone can find something of value here. But this book will be particularly useful for those who feel stuck. If you're trying to figure out why you're in this business, where it's going, or how to take it to the next level, I'm here to help.

Our field has unique considerations, and we can tackle them together, addressing ways to provide and convey value. Together, we'll cover the various aspects of the funeral, cemetery, and cremation businesses, addressing topics like how to determine whether to build or acquire a business, how to bring that funeral business into your culture to create a successful acquisition—especially when that means merging two families into one—and how to find the support necessary to navigate the current landscape. We'll also delve into what the future looks like, including the technology that will help the profession catch up to the rest of the world. With the knowledge that your commitment to care and quality has likely kept you in business from the start, we'll focus less on best practices and more on how to create a growth and customer-service mind-set that will help you make real progress, regardless of the stage you're in or the direction you're heading.

Ready to dig in? Let's start with a little history.

CHAPTER 1

Death and Taxes

For generations, funeral homes and cemeteries were exclusively a family affair—small businesses passed down along the same bloodline. But back in the 1960s, a funeral director named Robert Waltrip had an idea. He figured that if one could buy funeral homes within the same market, those businesses could share resources, create synergy, and be more profitable than they would be if they were operating on their own. This was the seed concept for Service Corporation International (SCI), which Waltrip founded in 1962.[2] The company began buying funeral homes across the country. SCI quickly gained traction and eventually went public in 1969.[3] Seeing their business boom, other acquisition companies subsequently opened with hopes of building similar success in the field.

From the '80s up until 2000, firms were taking an aggressive approach to acquisitions. It was a huge business. Owners were getting unjustifiable prices for their operations. Funeral homes and cemeteries that had been managed by families for generations were now being run by big corpora-

---

2   "About SCI." Service Corporation International. Accessed January 18, 2019. http://www.sci-corp.com/en-us/about-sci/our-business-history.page.

3   "SCI." Crunchbase. Accessed January 18, 2019. https://www.crunchbase.com/ipo/service-corp-international-ipo--c4d7684c#section-details.

tions from an office in Texas or Canada. While these corporations didn't necessarily have the profession-specific skills necessary to run the businesses properly, they did have the reporting right, and that helped them grow.

And then, around 1999 and 2000, it all just stopped. Acquisition companies either paused acquisitions to retool or went bankrupt. Suddenly, there were owners who wanted to sell but didn't have anyone to sell to. And while the funeral home or cemetery down the road may have been interested, because it's such a personal business, most owners weren't willing to sell to their neighbors. They feared their legacy would end right there.

Private buyers also faced another challenge after 2000: the cash flow–based finance companies that had been present in the '80s and '90s had virtually disappeared. Without them, it was very difficult for an individual owner to raise enough capital to buy another funeral home—especially if he or she was competing against a consolidator.

During that time, I noticed an interesting development when we were tasked to sell lists of firms owned by acquisition companies: while these lower-performing lists of funeral homes and cemeteries lost many at-need cases without the original owners and staff, their preneed business was intact. Even failing businesses owned by acquisition companies were still doing well with preneed sales that turned at-need. The companies knew that in the absence of good community contacts—like those built by long-standing family relationships—they could generate loyalty by going out to families and selling contracts that could be paid over time. It was a lesson for me on the importance of this type of sale for anyone in the profession. Of course, it's not why private owners get into the business; their primary purpose is to take care of families during some of the toughest times in their lives. But preneed sales provide significant value, because they help to lock in customers for the future.

In 2004, when I came on board to help helm Johnson Consulting, things were changing yet again. Acquisition companies that had bought up businesses wanted to divest from what they purchased during the funeral home and cemetery buying boom of the past two decades. With fewer additive businesses on their plates, acquisition companies were ready to buy in a more focused manner, exercising much better discipline in how they would come up with their EBITDAs, as well as the multiples they would pay. Today, that number reflects just how badly they want something, instead of their desire to compete for a piece of the pie.

Today's Challenges

The world continues to evolve, and though it may feel like it sometimes, the funeral, cemetery, and cremation professions are not exempt. While we may be slower than other fields to accept and integrate new developments, they're already here—and they will continue to arrive. To be successful in the future, we have to adapt. Let's discuss some of the changes affecting the profession today and tomorrow and the challenges they pose.

A Millennial Mind-Set

In the past, when it came to work, many people followed in the footsteps of their parents. They didn't know any better, and they didn't have anything called the internet to show them who they could be. Today, it's much easier to see all of the possibilities out there. Younger generations understand that they don't have to grind it out every day in a funeral home or cemetery where they're around death all the time and on call twenty-four seven. These professions are boring but steady—a reality that has appeal—but that also makes this work less exciting than, say, software development. Instead of taking over the family business, we are seeing young adults encourage their parents to cash out while they go on to do something else. They also want more life balance, so those who remain in the business are willing to outsource different functions, ones their parents may have been committed to handling themselves. They take care of the tasks in their wheelhouse and hire companies like mine for the other stuff. It goes without saying that my own professional coach challenges me to consider what I should be doing if my pay rate was $1,000 per hour. This provides good clarity on what my daily to-dos should be and who should be doing the rest of the work. To be sure, I feel like I can do it all; however, that is not the best use of my time and skill set.

Finding Good Help

In addition to the fact that our children are less interested in pursuing this line of work, finding good help is becoming more and more challenging. People would rather do something else than work in a funeral home or cemetery, where there's not much of a ladder. While an owner may be doing well, there can be little room for growth for managers or anyone else. Why? We've seen numerous instances where owners decide to sell their facilities, and managers who have been trained to take over are not interested in paying them a premium, because they have developed relationships with both staff and customers. If the owner won't accept their price, some feel they can open up their own enterprise and take those contacts with them. As such, owners keep key players in the dark to protect their connections—something quite contrary to more modern-day employee development concepts.

Rising Cremation Rates

While funeral business owners have been enjoying good profitability for the highly specialized services they provide, rising cremation rates create a new challenge. At my funeral home in Sun City, Arizona, where everyone is from somewhere else, cremation rate is around 80 percent. Rates across the US differ greatly, depending on the type and size of the community. But the reality is, everyone will get there. Discount cremation—something that is far more prevalent today than it was twenty years ago—has become a big part of the profession, adopted by almost every funeral home owner who said previously that it would never work. Further, if you are struggling to grow, the only option many funeral homes and cemeteries have to keep from getting, well, killed, is to either open up a direct cremation business or reduce expenses.

The Growing Role of Technology

It's been a slow creep, but in the near future, we are all going to have to face the changes technology is bringing to the field. Everyone will have to put their prices online. With that being the case, it will become necessary to differentiate yourself from the next funeral home or cemetery with an online explanation. But how do you describe your true value to your customers? How can you capture the worth of your facility and care you provide—large buildings with beautiful chapels and visitation rooms, a kind and caring staff, beautiful cemetery grounds, grief support, and more—online? And how do you convey all that to a customer who will only deal with death once or twice in his or her lifetime in the short period of time he or she has to make a decision?

The Result? Eroding Profitability

The collective effect of these changes is eroding profitability. Owners have to pay people more to keep them interested in the space—whether it's members of the next generation who'd rather pursue other fields or hired help who know there's not really anywhere to go. In fact, we have seen the benchmark for payroll costs as a percentage of net sales grow by almost 5 percent in the last few years.

Businesses that don't go the discount cremation route also have to compete against operations that do, further defining the value behind their prices. And those who do decide to add low-cost cremation will face another hurdle. Ironically, profitability with cremation is higher, but there are fewer dollars per cremation, meaning owners have to do more funerals or concede to having less cash coming in. But it's not all doom and gloom: there's plenty of opportunity if you find the right angle.

The Potential

While we may be boring, we're certainly steady. The fact of the matter is, outside of taxes, death is the only other guarantee in life. You can run, but you can't hide. You're going to need the services our profession provides at one point or another. That means there's a guaranteed list of customers for the foreseeable future. In the US, the death rate is .85 percent, which equates to about 2.7 million deaths every year.[4] And the death rate will only increase. Baby boomers are now entering old age. Ten thousand boomers are turning sixty-five every day, and the number of Americans aged sixty-five or older is projected to reach 88.5 million by 2050—more than double 2010's older adult population. While it may sound like a downer if you're part of this rapidly aging generation, it's certainly a boon for the funeral, cemetery, and cremation professions.[5]

Stability in an Unstable World

For investors looking for a reliable source of income, funeral homes and cemeteries provide solid options. As I look into buying funeral and cemetery operations and reach out to the investment community for support, I'm often struck by the fact that these firms are used to putting down money with little to no return for years, if at all. That's not the case with our profession. Funeral homes have some of the lowest failure rates of any small

4   "Deaths and Mortality." Centers for Disease Control and Prevention." CDC. May 2017. https://www.cdc.gov/nchs/fastats/deaths.htm.

5   Grayson Vincent and Victoria Velkoff, "The Next Four Decades: The Older Population in the United States: 2010 to 2050." U.S. Department of Commerce Economics and Statistics Administration. May 2010. {HYPERLINK "C:\\Users\\arielhubbard\\Downloads\\The Next Four Dec-ades.pdf"}.

business, with a Small Business Association (SBA) loan ten-year default rate of just 6.5 percent.[6] And most funeral homes have been operating since the late 1800s, making them more stable than most enterprises out there.

While you can't expect exponential growth, there's always business, meaning investors get an immediate return. In an environment where interest rates are nothing and people aren't sure where to put their money, investing in a funeral home and cemetery and making 6–10 percent from day one is quite attractive.

The field isn't affected by recessions either. Whether Mom dies in an up economy or a down one, I've got to use a funeral business, and I'm probably not going to change my mind about what I was going to get for her, especially if she's already prefunded her funeral. In fact, in some areas, business may be even busier—fortunately or unfortunately, depending on how you look at it.

> *When it comes to managing some of the toughest moments in their lives, they go somewhere they trust.*

The Opportunity to Provide Care

Is it sexy? No. Dealing with death every day can be depressing. But we all know how rewarding it can be to take care of families and make a tough situation better. In that sense, we're making a real difference. And our dedication pays off: families come back. When it comes to managing some of the toughest moments in their lives, they go somewhere they trust. That contributes to the success of privately owned businesses and of corporate ones with good management.

---

6   Jackie Zimmerman, "SBA Loan Defaults Mirror US Economy, Consumer Tastes." NerdWallet. October 2017. https://www.nerdwallet.com/blog/small-business/ sba-lending-trends-match-consumer-tastes/.

Slow, Manageable Progress

In addition, the changes aren't happening all at once. They're very slow; you can anticipate what's coming down the line. You have plenty of time to train up and turn issues into opportunities. If you're prepared, you're good at follow-through, and you maintain the capacity as a business owner and manager to adopt new strategies that take into account changes in the profession, you'll put yourself in a good position to weather any challenges and come out on top. It's all about people and process. Being a good leader, building a staff you can count on, and creating systems in which your team can comfortably operate will contribute to your success—as will putting yourself out in the community and meeting with the residents you may serve someday. I can't stress enough the importance of preparation. All of what I just said can be true for day-to-day success; however, you must consider always putting yourself in a ready position to take opportunities for growth when you are presented with them. They don't come every day; however, it's amazing how much more frequently opportunities are presented to you when you are organized and prepared! There's also the potential for innovation.

A Chance to Break the Mold

Today, there's a place in the market for death care businesses that doesn't involve funeral homes and cemeteries—especially since there are plenty of people out there who would be happy to avoid them entirely. I recently held an open house at my funeral home, marketing it through Facebook and bringing the target demographics down to thirty years old just to see what kind of turnout we'd get. We didn't quite capture the younger crowd—we are in Sun City, after all, where nearly 80 percent of the population is sixty-five or older and the median age is seventy-five—but we did have about two hundred people show up. At first, most of them were somewhat mortified, creeping in as if they were entering a haunted house before they saw that there was nothing to it. The fact of the matter is that although all of us will deal with death at some point, the majority of people don't ever want to think about it. America is considered a "death-denying culture." Grief counselor, educator, and founder of the Center for Loss and Life Transition, Dr. Alan Wolfelt explains, "Especially in Western cultures, people tend to believe that unhappiness is a bad thing. We think that suffering should be avoided, and if we do encounter it, it's our right to put it behind us as soon as we can."[7] As a profession, we can embrace that mentality and provide customers with an experience that departs—pardon the pun—from the traditional funeral home or cemetery experience.

There are all kinds of ways to innovate in this space and attract the many customers who aren't very comfortable with the concept of mortality. You may not want to go as far as turning remains into diamonds or launching them into space, but creating a facility with a modern feel that doesn't immediately conjure up associations with the end—perhaps a glass building with concrete floors—may be a way to break the mold and tap into a new market.

The Role of Growth

Growth is a factor in increasing your potential too—though it's often overlooked. I'm part of two different business networks, one for entrepreneurs and another for funeral businesses. The difference between the groups is striking. In my entrepreneurship group, we talk about our companies' current and future growth constantly. Everyone is plotting his or her next move. But in the funeral business group, growth is not the leading discussion. Most participants have succumbed to the facts that their market includes a certain number of deaths per year and that they'll receive a particular percentage of that business. They talk about how they can offer

---

7   Alan Wolfelt, "Common Misconceptions." Batesville. Accessed February 15, 2019. https://www.batesville.com/common-misconceptions/.

more value to a customer who doesn't really understand the value of their service to begin with—highlighting that as their primary challenge—but the conversation ends there.

It's crucial to remember that it's possible—and often necessary—to shift to a growth mind-set. For example, while eroding profitability creates multiple challenges, it also provides numerous opportunities, including the potential to acquire your competition. If you do, you'll be better prepared for changing consumer preferences, such as an increasing demand for cremation. And with the knowledge that cremation rates are rising, you can harness that as a route for growth. After all, have you ever thought that if your cremation rate is low, perhaps that means there are more cremations you can get? At my funeral business in Sun City, we recently changed the sign to include "Cremation Center." While I was reviewing the sign with my landscaper, he thought that we were just now getting into cremation since we were adding cremation to our name. We already had 80 percent cremation when he said that!

With these factors in mind, let's explore the life cycle of the funeral, cemetery, and cremation businesses and the decisions that can help you foster more value and possibilities each step of the way.

CHAPTER 2

The Life Cycle of Death Care

It's hard to have a conversation about the funeral and cemetery professions without mentioning Todd Van Beck. Todd has been a name in the business forever (or since 1973—whichever seems longer to you). A certified funeral service practitioner, embalmer, dean of the College of Funeral Management at the University of Memphis, and the author of four books and four hundred articles, Todd has seen and done it all in our sector. When speaking to a group of funeral and cemetery professionals, he often poses the same question: "What is it that we do for families when they come to our businesses?"

Some attendees mention the nuts and bolts: administration, making funeral arrangements, embalming, digging the grave, or directing. Others go for the bigger, softer picture, saying that we help grieving families. But Todd breaks it down to one single point: we're solving a problem. Someone has died and the family needs to handle it.

It's a good point to make. How each of us handles that death makes the experience more or less meaningful for the family, but the bottom line is that they have a problem and they need our professional help to solve it.

In fact, the funeral business was built by entrepreneurial ambulance drivers and furniture makers who realized that they could help families address an upsetting but very real problem: taking people who had died and—for lack of a better phrase—disposing of them. With their existing skills, those clever individuals found a solution. Ambulance drivers moved the bodies to where they needed to be, and furniture makers began building caskets.

How each of us handles that death makes the experience more or less meaningful for the family, but the bottom line is that they have a problem and they need our professional help to solve it.

Today, funeral businesses help with the legal portion of this process too: getting the necessary permits, whether for cremation, burial, or shipping, and processing death certificates. While things have gotten a bit more complex since the days when drivers and carpenters did double duty, one thing remains the same. In this profession, as we attempt to negotiate the logistics of death, we face an added challenge: grief and loss. The people tasked with answering a family's call are trying to provide the best customer experience they can, knowing the person on the other line is handling one of the worst times in their life.

Those who ran funeral homes and cemeteries back in the day figured that, to meet that need, their facilities should match the general mood. They built somber places, dark to mirror the experience of the families walking through their doors. While many funeral and cemetery businesses are remodeling to create beautiful spaces reflective of the fact that funerals can be celebrations of life, no one *wants* to come to one—yet another problem with its own set of burgeoning solutions, which we'll discuss in greater detail throughout this book. But first, let's take a quick look at how these businesses solve the primary issue at hand: getting a body from the location of expiration to its final resting place—wherever that may be.

The Life Cycle of the Funeral, Cemetery, and Cremation Businesses

Paperwork and Preparation

After death, the first place most people go is to a funeral home/mortuary or cemetery. In addition to the preparation of bodies for burial or cremation, this part of the process involves something many problems begin with: paperwork. Funeral home and cemetery staff handle it all, including documentation, permitting, and processing death certificates.

As you may know all too well, death certificates—those documents none of us really consider until someone has died—can be tricky things. They serve as a reminder that a problem many of us encounter while we're living, that no one believes you are who you say you are without proof, continues even in death. As such, that death certificate becomes essential. It's necessary to process life insurance, demonstrate to utility companies that accounts need to be changed over, and so much more. And getting ahold of that crucial form is a problem few people could solve without the help of funeral businesses.

But the challenge doesn't stop there. Because our businesses rely on state governments, we're far more behind than other sectors, and we're often dealing with actual paper. If your business is in one of the states that has not yet switched over to electronic filing, and you don't report the right cause of death, you're going to find yourself hunting down a doctor for a signature. It's amazing that such a simple-sounding process can be so difficult. But if you're deep in the weeds of death paperwork, and you learn that the heart attack a person had moments before he died isn't necessarily what killed him, you're also on the hook for tracking down a doctor to provide the final answer. In most states, that death certificate, once signed, has to be submitted to the local health department and approved to allow for disposition of the deceased.

Funeral homes and mortuaries are also processing life insurance claims, insomuch as they're valid and will pay for the funeral itself. Ensuring that payment is made in full before services are rendered, either through an insurance policy, a prefunded funeral, or cash or check from the family, is particularly important, because in this business, there is no real recourse. You can't really reverse a burial—and certainly not cremation. If the service has already been rendered and you haven't collected payment, you've essentially met your end as far as that sale goes.

Funeral arrangers are tasked with handling any logistics with the family. They're collecting vital statistic information for permitting; learning a family's wishes as to whether they want their loved one buried or cremated; and presenting the family with available products, such as urns, caskets, and vaults. They're also finding out whether the body is going to a cemetery, and if so, which one. Arrangers are almost like wedding coordinators, making sure all of this stuff happens so when the day comes to memorialize that life, no one's worried about what kind of casket Grandpa will be buried in. In some cases, funeral directors will take over from there, handling the logistics of any visitations, services, or memorials so that it all goes off without a hitch.

In larger organizations, everything is specialized. A separate administrator will handle the death certificates and permitting, and embalmers will do only that: embalm. Occasionally, there's a separate staff member who just handles cremations as well. Meanwhile, in smaller funeral businesses, there is far more overlap. Funeral arrangers sometimes play the role of funeral director and vice versa. And in roughly 80 percent of organizations that hold 110 or fewer funerals a year, it's not unusual to find owners themselves wearing every hat—serving as funeral arranger, director, and embalmer. Some contract with removal companies to bring bodies in, while others handle even that task on their own. Because a single person is doing so many jobs in these small organizations, there's a lot of commitment involved. Death doesn't work on a schedule. There are lots of missed baseball games, recitals, and events and many late nights.

The crazy hours, hard labor, and less-than-sunshiny topic have younger generations asking why they'd do all of this work for so little compensation. Of course, it's all relative, since an owner may find him- or herself with two or three consecutive death-free days to do what they want—although it's hard not to begin worrying about when the next person will die so you can pay your bills.

Burial and Placement

For those who won't be cremated and set on a mantel, stored in a keepsake, spread over the ocean, or sent into orbit, cemeteries are the next stop. Administrators handle paperwork about placement—whether bodies or remains are going into the ground, a mausoleum, or a columbarium. The process of actually placing the remains is either outsourced to a vault company or handled internally by the grounds crew. At big cemeteries, there are teams tasked with overseeing different aspects of operations and maintenance—opening and closing teams, grounds maintenance teams, and irrigation teams, to name a few. The larger a cemetery is, the more complex its organizational chart. When funeral homes or mortuaries are located on the grounds of a cemetery, the burden of paperwork is combined—everything from permitting to plotting is managed in-house.

Aftercare

Aftercare occurs after the funeral or memorial service ends and the burial, placement, or shipment of remains is complete. This part of the process begins with family follow-ups—owners or employees reaching out to families to find out how the funeral or service went and gathering any additional information necessary for death certificates or life insurance. The next step is to find out if the family would find it valuable to prefund a funeral to avoid some of the financial strain that can occur when there isn't a plan in place to manage such a large expense all at once. After all, funeral professionals are providing essential solutions, but we never said it was cheap.

If the organization is big enough, aftercare is divided into two divisions—what we call a two-up system—in which the arranger does their part and a preneed family service counselor, who has also helped with the arrangement, receives the handoff to deliver the death certificates, talks about preneed arrangements, and stays in touch with the family.

Community counselors are also present in the space. Often contracted through insurance companies, these professionals are tasked solely with writing prefunded funerals in the community. They're out there knocking on doors, calling phone numbers, and hosting lunch-and-learns to get people thinking about and planning for death. Those who do well can be promoted to family service counselors—a highly coveted role since it doesn't require pounding the pavement in quite the same way. They're being handed families that have just gone through the process and are ready to talk about the benefits of prefunding a funeral.

A healthy book of preneed funerals remains a critical part of running a successful business today. For every preneed that comes due, there should be a new preneed being written. At the average funeral home, 35 percent of preneeds are turning at-need each year. At a one-hundred-call funeral home, that means you have to make up those thirty-five calls.

Why is it so important to keep booking preneeds? Think back to the early 2000s, when the funeral profession went into a tailspin. You'll remember that writing preneed funerals kept some acquisition businesses alive when many of them were dropping like flies. We saw then that even if funeral businesses were failing, with the number of calls diminishing each year, preneed sales remained steady. If, for example, you had a one-hundred-call business doing thirty-five preneed funerals annually, even when it became a fifty-call business, thirty-five of those calls were still preneed.

Since preneeds are so important, having family service and community counselors can be crucial to a business's success. Funeral arrangers and directors are, by their very nature, caregivers. They're not salespeople. But these counselors are. Moreover, they can balance the caregiving qualities necessary to support a family after the death of a loved one with the sales aspect. These roles also provide a layer of defense if the other funeral home or cemetery in town has a community counselor out there writing preneeds. Why? If competition ends up writing one for a family that would have otherwise used your services, that business is gone … and technically speaking, so is the enterprise value benefit of $20,000 associated with that family!

Despite the value of these roles, most funeral businesses don't want to put a counselor on their payroll full time. Many believe it's too great a financial burden to bear. Instead, they challenge their insurance companies to manage that person and have them paid through commissions. And yet, the same businesses often complain that it's difficult, if not impossible, to grow. I have to say, the irony just kills me. But so many funeral professionals have certain cash-flow expectations. They've adjusted to the lifestyle they have, and they haven't challenged themselves to think about how to reinvest in their businesses to help them grow. Putting more money back into the business—in this case, by hiring a full-time counselor—means sacrificing some of the cash they've been able to take home. They want to grow, but they tell themselves that their current MO is just representative of how funeral businesses are run. Until the mind-set shifts and owners begin investing in their businesses, many of us are pretty much embodying the definition of insanity: doing the same thing over and over again and expecting a different result.

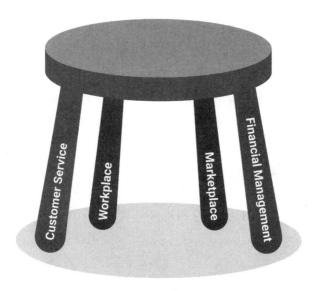

The Four-Legged Stool

With the understanding that some of your current practices may not be serving you, let's examine what we at Johnson Consulting consider to be four primary areas that will benefit from your attention. We call this model the four-legged stool. Why? Each area plays an essential part in keeping the business upright. When one leg is missing, or even wobbly, everything else suffers and you're at risk of falling flat on your rump.

Customer Service

Customer service is a very important measure, and it begins with the culture you breed in the office. At Johnson Consulting, we take the pulse on customer service whenever we go into a business and measure it as we progress.

We frequently consult *The Power of Moments: Why Certain Experiences Have Extraordinary Impact,* by Chip and Dan Heath, which is "written for anyone who cares about improving the experience of others," according to the authors.[8] In their book, Chip and Dan discuss the moments that stand out in people's minds: "peak experiences" and endings. The death of a loved one, in a sense, has the potential to be both. If you can deliver exceptional customer service during one of the most difficult endings any of us will experience, you can make the moments they spend with you stand out for the better.

To begin analyzing your customer service, think about how things are handled when they go wrong. It's easy to say "that's not my fault," and it may very well be true. But whether or not it's your fault, it's still your problem. You can also ask questions about the quality of the experience you provide. For example, how are your service and employee handoffs? Are they warm or cold?

Rather than leaning solely on self-report to get a sense of whether you're providing exceptional customer service, *ask*. You should be surveying your customers to determine the quality of the service you provide. It's amazing how many funeral home owners and managers don't survey their customers. Quite honestly, I think it's because they don't want the feedback. They feel that they're working hard;

Until the mind-set shifts and owners begin investing in their businesses, many of us are pretty much embodying the definition of insanity: doing the same thing over and over again and expecting a different result.

they're doing everything they're supposed to do. If the customer doesn't like it, that's too bad. But the fact of the matter is, it's just an excuse. Surveying

8   Dan Schwabel, "Dan and Chip Heath: How to Create Powerful Moments at Work." *Forbes*. October 2017. https://www.forbes.com/sites/danschawbel/2017/10/03/dan-and-chip-heath-how-to-create-powerful-moments-at-work/#20a7b75a6efd.

customers and asking tough questions are essential to producing those peak moments and preventing your business from kicking the bucket.

Workplace

The next leg is your workplace. Here, we're talking about the structure and organization of your business. One critical aspect of this leg is communication, because—as with most things in life—it is at the core of a business's success. To evaluate the sturdiness of this leg, you can ask some of the following questions:

- What does the organizational chart look like?
- How do things get done?
- What is the culture? Do you survey staff members and get their opinions at least annually, or have you created a workplace environment based solely on your own idea of what it should be like?
- How is information communicated?
- Is there a good flow from death to first call and beyond? Do you survey your employees to get their judgment on this as well?

Marketplace

The marketplace is a big deal for any business, and certainly for the funeral and cemetery businesses, since so much goodwill is involved. It's easy to get stuck in our day-to-day jobs and forget to pay attention to the future. It takes time and energy to determine whether we're in the right location, or what the marketplace looks like and whether we're positioned to succeed—not just this year or next, but five or ten years from now. However, it's crucial to consider the current and future environment, to ask tough questions. And when you do, you also have to pay attention to the answers. Here are just a handful of the questions you should be asking when attempting to uncover insights about your place in the market:

- Do people know your name?

- How is your market share?
- Are you the leader in your area?
- How is your pricing in relation to others?
- Is your business growing or declining?
- What about your location? Are you in the path of progress, or do you stand to lose some ground in the next five years?

It may be difficult to dig deep and find the answers you need—especially if they're not the ones you want. But it's the only way to make sure you're on track to accomplish your goals, whatever they are. Throughout the years, I've had the chance to talk to successful entrepreneurs in other businesses sectors, and a key difference arises: they find ways to get the hard-to-find answers. Why? They know those discoveries are key in helping them figure out how to be unique or inventive in their marketplace. They have the tenacity and grit to dig deep into how each of the players in the market is doing what they do and how to differentiate. This seems critical to success, and to do it, you really need to look outside the box!

Financial Management

Last—and perhaps most important—is the financial piece. If you make sure the other legs are strong and sturdy, this one should fall right into place. My father has always said, "If you take care of families, they'll take care of you." In the funeral business, there's a lot of truth to that. It's hard to just break into this business, or even to expand into a new community. But once you're in and you've established some goodwill, the network that you've built will return the favor.

To truly care for your community, you have to recognize that preferences are changing—and adapt to those changes. Some funeral professionals take these shifts personally. They believe that if families are choosing one option over another, such as direct cremation over burial, they don't care to memorialize their loved ones. The fact is that customers just have different ideas on how they want to handle death. It's not a reflection on you or your business. The system is still the same: funeral professionals take care of those families, and the families take care of them. It's just about determining what it means to provide that care in the first place.

That translates to the financials, and it all starts with budgeting. Though it can be intimidating, it's not hard—and it can actually be pretty fun if you do it correctly. But it's not a part you can skip if you want to be profitable. You have to look at how your revenue comes in, how it is created, what your case mix looks like, your average sale amount, and how your pricing is affecting your sales.

Next, it's time to think about expenses. Are you benchmarking them against other professionals in your space? Doing so is an invaluable way to determine if your labor, advertising, cost of goods, and more are where they should be.

Below are some of the typical benchmarks we see at Johnson Consulting. The numbers are percentages of net sales (they don't include cash advances or accommodation revenues). They don't include any owner-related expenses either—this is what things should look like if you went to live on an island and your business continued to operate on its own.

- Payroll: 28–33 percent (this is roughly 5 percent higher at a cemetery depending on the size and complexity of the grounds maintenance)
- Overall EBITDA (owner adjusted): 25–39 percent (for a cemetery, this can be dramatically lower or higher by up to 5–10 percent depending on the complexity of the grounds maintenance and the volume of preneed sales)
- Cost of goods: 13–15 percent (typically less for a cemetery as the costs are on the balance sheet as they are constructed ahead of the sale)
- Facility: 7–10 percent (if you're renting, add another 6–12 percent to this section, for a total of 13–22 percent on the high end)
- Other G&A: 7–10 percent

- Advertising: 3–4 percent
- Vehicles: 3 percent

It's crucial to review your budget and expenses and make adjustments. You have to make sure that at the end of the year, you're going to have some additional cash to put back into the business. Why? If you don't keep your facilities up to date and reinvest in your organization in other ways, the marketplace leg of your stool begins to shake.

Keeping the Legs of the Stool Sturdy

It quickly becomes apparent how interdependent the legs of your stool are, along with areas of your business that may affect more than one leg. For instance, staffing falls into both customer service and financials. If you're overstaffed, it's costing you a lot of money to have people just sitting around. If you're understaffed, your customer service suffers, potentially leading to fewer sales. Thus, it's crucial to make sure all of your legs are working together to keep your business running.

Life-and-Death Decisions

With an understanding of the areas that affect businesses most, it's time to take a good, hard look at your own operation and make some decisions about what you want your future to look like—and how to get there. Changes are coming to our profession whether we want them to or not, and it's up to us to adjust or face the consequences. Let's run through some of the decisions you will have make in the near future, if you haven't already.

Do You Want to Maintain Your Lifestyle or Generate Growth?

Right off the bat, owners are faced with a big-picture decision: Are you in the business because it simply fuels your existence, or are you here to grow and make the corresponding investments necessary for future success? Growth starts with a well-thought-out strategic plan that takes into account the present and future of the funeral business, along with a budget that delineates the investments you need to make to meet your goals.

If you're just a lifestyle guy (or gal), you may argue that none of that is important. You simply focus on keeping your costs low and enjoy life. At the moment, the funeral business allows for that, because profit margins are high. For example, if you owned a restaurant that pulled in $1 million per year, you'd hardly be profitable. Meanwhile, a $1 million funeral home is likely very profitable. Even a $500,000-revenue funeral home can provide a very nice living.

When it comes to lifestyle versus growth, there is no right or wrong answer. If it's all about the lifestyle for you, though, you do have to accept that you may lose market share over time to those willing to invest in their own growth. And please note: some adaptation is still necessary. Some of the changes coming down the pipeline are ones that customers will begin to expect. Cremation options, an online presence, and other buyer-driven demands are becoming par for the course in the market. If you choose to do nothing, it may indeed be a death sentence for your business at some point. After all, as with jumping out of an airplane, it's not the jump that kills you—it's the impact when you hit the ground.

So stare deep into that crystal ball and ask yourself where you want to be five years from now. If the answer is right where you are today, what are you doing to secure the current lifestyle for the future? If you want to be bigger—to have more equity value in your business—what are you doing to make that happen?

Will You Get Online or Get Lost in the Shuffle?

Another decision—and it's a big one—is how to handle the new presence of online customers. Everyone's in a rush these days. We're all guilty of it. And for families, the prospect of going in and meeting with an arranger, spending time in that building they don't want to be in, handling something they don't want to handle for one and a half to two and a half hours (even longer if they need to go to a cemetery), and then paying immediately—which may pose a real financial challenge—certainly does not put the "fun" in "funeral."

A reasonable solution, particularly for the younger customers out there? Sidestepping some of the death-induced discomfort and taking care of all the arrangements online. In fact, many younger people wouldn't understand—or even believe—me if I told them they couldn't take care of this with a few clicks of a mouse. For anyone who's interested in more than just the lifestyle, or even just ensuring they can maintain their current station in the future, there's a big push to get online.

There are additional hurdles out there that are about more than just cultivating a digital presence. One of the effects of this shift is the commoditization of the highly personal service funeral professionals provide. This is a point of contention for so many people in the business. They got into it for the right reasons. They're here to take care of families. It's a noble cause, involving a level of service that is often as intangible as it is invaluable—one that everyone should know more about. Unfortunately, fewer customers are interested in hearing your spiel these days. They just want to know what your prices are and make a decision from there.

This change has allowed businesses with very minimal facilities and offerings to pop up online, with prices that are hard to beat. Despite the fact that the customer will most likely get what they pay for, because they're visiting our businesses maybe twice in their life, the importance of that personal connection is lost in translation. Just as a note, my consulting company receives tens of thousands of customer surveys each year, and the lowest satisfaction ratings come from those customers that choose direct cremation. Sounds like a message your future customers need to hear!

Of course, since roughly 80 percent of funeral businesses are in small towns, it will take longer for these shifts to take full effect. In the town of Batesville, Indiana, for instance, residents still drive past the local funeral home on Pearl Street to see who died and decide whether or not to crash the visitation. But in other areas—especially bigger ones—that just isn't happening anymore. Funeral business owners are losing some of the mayoral status they once held, along with market share.

To Buy or to Sell?

Some owners have already recognized the changes headed their way and embraced them—or have at least chosen to address them. They may be considering starting a direct cremation business, all while wondering whether it will affect their traditional operations, their families, the legacies they've built, and their existing equity.

Some are deciding to simply sell and cash out, so that they can avoid any necessary revamping. Still others are determining whether they should buy more businesses to put the competition—which may be unwilling or unable to address these changes—out of business. Deciding whether to buy or sell based on coming market conditions may seem like a dismal scenario. But, as we've established, those challenges always bring with them opportunities for greater success. I see plenty of examples of funeral homes out there that have built online cremation businesses, posted their prices online, and found ways to innovate (more on that in a bit) and are thriving as a result.

How Will You Handle Rising Cremation Rates?

Cremation is another hot topic—not just literally, but figuratively. We know those rates are rising, and businesses will have to decide whether to cultivate that portion of their business or merge. However, there's a bit more time to wrap our heads around this one. Why? With boomers rapidly approaching old age, deaths are also steadily increasing. For a while, we may assume that those rates will help counterbalance cremation's growing popularity—but not forever.

There are also real estate considerations to take into account. If more people are choosing direct cremation, and thus holding fewer services, what happens to your existing space? Say you have a big, beautiful building meant to house ceremonies—chapel and all. If fewer people are interested in memorializing their loved ones with a big gathering, would it make sense to move to a smaller space? Or is the space you have serving your population fine, and all it requires is an update to reflect more modern considerations—adding a few windows to lighten things up, for instance?

Crematories and Cremation

As of 2019, the cremation rate in the United States is projected to be 54.8 percent, making cremation the disposition method of choice for more than half of the population.[9] You can certainly outsource it, but there's something nice about being in control of your own destiny—at least in my book. There is also significant perceived value in saying that you own a crematory. When you do, you'll be telling the family that they'll never leave your care, and when they're dealing with loss, few things are more comforting.

Of course, there is homework to be done. You have to check your zoning and find out whether you can even have a crematory on your property before jumping over any hurdles necessary to get approval. And because you're putting a body through an irreversible process, there's more litigation with cremation than anything else in our space. You're dealing with anything that's going into the retort along with the body—the hazard

---

9   Brigit Katz, "Cremation Rates Reach All-Time High in the U.S." Smithsonian.com. August 2017. https://www.smithsonianmag.com/smart-news/cremation-rates-reach-all-time-high-us-180964478/.

of medical devices, the issue of jewelry. There are so many signatures required. And it doesn't happen often, but you have to understand that the person lying there isn't telling you what their name is, and you probably haven't met them before. You certainly don't want to put the wrong person through the process. That's why it's crucial to have an ID view, confirmation from the family. Some religions even require that a family member is present. In fact, sometimes they want to push the button themselves. But if you have control over all of these aspects, you can put families more at ease, increasing the chances they'll choose you. And there are plenty of resources out there to help you make sure you're covering yourself on the off chance that something does happen. Crematory manufacturing companies can help you navigate it all.

Of course, offering cremation on site doesn't fit every business's needs. You have to determine whether you do enough cremations to justify it. That depends on how much you're charging for each one. Perhaps you don't do enough cremations on your own, but it would make sense to enter a collective and share resources among a few businesses in your area. For example, my funeral business maintains a relationship with other private funeral homes in town. We've entered into a partnership of sorts, running a crematory that's not on our premises but very much a part of our family based on those who use it and those who don't. As such, we're able to reassure our customers that they're in the best hands, without having to shoulder the responsibility of operating a crematory all on our own. Since, in the end, I always consider the value impact of a decision, I like to run the following exercise, which may help you decide whether a retort is right for you.

Consider what it may cost to purchase a crematory unit. Let's say the cost to you is going to be $85,000–$100,000. (If you purchase a Facultatieve unit, it will be much more, but what an awesome crematory unit! Check it out.) Now let's assume you have two hundred cremations a year and it is costing you $350 per cremation, or $70,000 a year. If you are to have your own crematory, certainly that cost will drop greatly; your new costs, of course, being most likely utilities and labor. Let's say in the end your net cost reduction is $20,000 (could be more or less depending on your situation). Now take that $20,000 and multiply it by a hypothetical enterprise value of six times. That means you add $120,000 in enterprise value by owning your own crematory. And certainly if the cremation numbers are higher, then the savings are even more!

How Do You Find Balance?

There are also a number of decisions to be made in order to find balance—or some semblance thereof. It's a challenge all professionals run into, no matter the industry: calibrating business, family, and personal life and hoping not to lose our minds in the process. The next generation of funeral business owners tends to care more about this than their predecessors. They want to know how they can create as much balance as they can—something that can be difficult when your business involves being on call—and it often affects their decision to stay in the profession or move on.

I've learned that true balance is just not realistic. Things will always tip in one direction or another. All you can do is be cognizant of that reality and try to level things out as best you can. One of the ways to do that is through succession planning.

You may decide, for instance, that someday you'd like to retire and have your manager eventually run the company. But many of us know that for funeral business owners, this is a particularly challenging proposition. In organizations or locations that may often have a maximum of five people, the "corporate ladder" is pretty darn short. If one staff member has an entrepreneurial mind and wants to make the climb, there are a few issues to contend with. For one, they aren't automatically qualified—or suited—for any open roles. A funeral director doesn't necessarily make a good arranger, and vice versa. And neither of those automatically make a good manager. Further, a manager isn't always fit to be an owner.

And in a field where so much goodwill is involved, how do we position employees to take over the organization and lift some of the burden without allowing them to steal all of our customers? In a major market like Las Vegas or Los Angeles, the owner doesn't necessarily have a presence in the community. But in a town like Batesville, Indiana, owners can be ingrained in the community. Everyone in town calls them on their cell phone or at home when death comes knocking. How do you even attempt balance by leaning on your team without giving up the personal relationships you've built? If you're not careful, your once-trusted director could easily decide that they don't need you anymore and set up a competing operation.

If you want to avoid that potential by selling to your employees directly, things get a little more complicated—and we see it all the time at Johnson Consulting. Our clients really want to sell to their staff, but the staff members often don't have the money to buy the whole operation. With relatively meager incomes and a banking system that doesn't understand our sector, it can be very difficult for them to get business loan that would cover the cost.

But it's pretty easy to get a real estate loan. That funeral director or manager may be able to buy a building. And, if you haven't played your cards right—and he doesn't accept your price—he can take some of your contacts with him, putting you in the very situation you were hoping to avoid.

What Will Your Retirement Look Like?

Retirement is a factor too. Your funeral or cemetery business is likely the most valuable asset you have. If your most valuable asset was in the form of a stock, you'd probably look at that stock value pretty frequently—maybe even on a daily basis, and at least on a quarterly or annual basis. But many of the owners I know don't have a clue what the value of their business is, despite the fact that this knowledge is crucial to making decisions, setting goals, and planning for life after work.

You have to have some idea of where you are currently and where you want to be in order to plan for tomorrow. Instead, people have the tendency to believe everything will work out on its own. They imagine they will identify and accomplish their goals through osmosis. That's a great way to look at adversity, but a less-than-stellar approach to take when it comes to your future. To make sure you can enjoy life for as many years as you've got, you have to start with the end in mind and work backward.

So many of us just focus on whatever's in front of our faces. (Which, ironically, is a suggested solution to fighting depression. Anxiety? Not so much.) We don't look out far enough. But our success is always going to be limited by our vision. As such, you have to determine what success looks like to you and broaden your gaze to match. Maybe it's not about money—maybe it's about the number of hours you work, or the time you want to spend with your kids, or the ways you'd like to contribute to your community. All of these are relevant and important to your decision-making process, but until you get a handle on what your ideal path looks like, it's going to be very hard to make any progress on it. There's a popular line in the original *Alice's Adventures in Wonderland* that my dad has used when describing the need to identify your path: "One day Alice came to a fork in the road and saw a Cheshire cat in a tree. 'Which road do I take?' she asked. 'Where do you want to go?' was his response. 'I don't know,' Alice answered. 'Then,' said the cat, 'it doesn't matter.'"

The first step in taking control of your future is to get a business valuation. If your business is not worth what you thought it was, the company conducting the valuation can tell you why, and you can address those issues directly—preparing yourself so when it's time to retire, you can.

We've covered the basics when it comes to the life cycle and structure of funeral and cemetery businesses, as well as the pressing decisions that owners will face, not necessarily today but certainly in the years to come. Building or buying a new business may seem like the next logical step, whether it's your first foray into ownership or you're thinking about adding to an existing operation. In the next chapter, we'll look at the factors to consider when a new business is on the table.

CHAPTER 3

From the Ground Up: Starting or Buying a Funeral or Cemetery Business

Starting a funeral or cemetery business isn't easy. Why? Death has been around for, well, eternity. For as long as our ancestors have been able to use tools and build structures, some semblance of funeral homes, cemeteries, and crematoriums have been around. As such, there's almost guaranteed to be a funeral or cemetery business in every market. They say there's a profession that's been around just as long, but that's for a different book.

You can imagine that the prospect of building a new funeral home or cemetery to compete against one that has been in existence for one hundred years or more is a little difficult. It's not like starting a new restaurant or something. A community can usually make room for more pancakes, but it's hard to drum up the same kind of goodwill that funeral businesses— and especially cemeteries—are built on. That said, starting a new business is far from impossible, and there are certainly good reasons to do so. Here are just a few:

- Playing defense: Maybe there's a market that has grown in recent years and is currently underserved. Perhaps you're serving some of that market from an adjacent town, but it's just a matter of time before someone sets up shop and takes that business from you—not because the families don't like you, but because it's just more convenient. Building a new facility to beat them to it may be a good plan.

- Playing offense: Perhaps you're on the offensive side of this equation: you see a growing and underserved market, currently managed in part by a business with limited resources. You have the opportunity to come in and build something new before the competition gets legs in the situation.

- Meeting the needs of a growing population: Perhaps your market is experiencing significant growth. Starting a new business or adding to an existing one may be the right way to go. If this scenario is similar to your own, it is important to keep in mind that in the past, when burials took up a larger share of the market, owners had the potential to cover their costs a little quicker since the cost per sale was relatively high. With today's higher cremation rates, you have to be a bit more careful, since they bring in less revenue than burials.

If you have an existing business and you're thinking about branching out, remember that with any new opportunity come new considerations. One of the things I've seen over the course of my journey, both buying funeral businesses myself and helping others buy and sell, is that funeral business owners tend to make the same mistakes. They see an opportunity in an adjacent town and decide to build a business just like their existing one. But that business doesn't necessarily work for the customers in their new market, or they take too long to build a client base that will pay for the debt they incurred. With tons of debt they may have never had before— especially if their original organization has been around for generations— they're forced to sell everything. You can avoid a similar fate. But it does take some planning and prudence. Your first order of business: to make sure your existing operation is in line.

Getting Your House—or Funeral/ Cemetery Business—in Order

Before starting something new, it is imperative to make sure your current business is successful. You should prepare to build or buy a business in the same way you would if you were going to sell. That means being well strategized in each area of the four-legged stool. The business you currently have should be operating well, with a team that works like a well-oiled machine, clean financials, and a budget that you treat like the Bible. Those are the businesses that get the best value. When you're ready to sell, you're usually ready to buy or start a new enterprise. Your organization is operating at peak

> *The business you currently have should be operating well, with a team that works like a well-oiled machine, clean financials, and a budget that you treat like the Bible.*

efficiency, giving you the bandwidth to branch out to another location without sacrificing anything in your present workflow.

If your house—or funeral home/cemetery, as the case may be—isn't in order, you'll find that you're stretching yourself and your staff too thin. Any existing disorganization will become even more disorganized. If any success comes your way, it will be based on luck alone. In this case, betting your livelihood is probably not a gamble you should take. But if everything is in good shape, it's time to develop a thorough understanding of what you're getting yourself into.

Buy or Build?

If you're thinking about buying a business, the same things that prepare you to sell are important to consider. What does the business's current budget look like? How about the staff? Would the employees leave or retire if that business were to sell, or is there a good succession plan in place? At Johnson Consulting, we use a formula to determine whether a particular business might be a good buy. Funnily enough, it's the same one we use to determine whether a business is ready to sell—check out the JCG Value Matrix in chapter 9 for the rundown.

Maybe building something new seems like a better option, because you see a new market opportunity where nothing currently exists—or one that isn't being served to its full potential. It's important to look before you leap: you have to think not just about the number of families available in that market, but also the number with whom you have a real chance of doing business. It's usually a good idea to hire a company to perform a market study, as it is the best way to spend some money before you *really* spend your money. That way, you can ask those in the area whether they are looking for another funeral service option, just to get a feel of how many families you may be able to bring in. But there are two sides to this coin. On the one hand, you're getting feedback directly from the community—a significant perk. On the other, the community doesn't necessarily know what it needs, especially when it comes to a service they (hopefully, for their sake) won't be using too regularly. Do the survey but take it for what it's worth. Just because someone says they would choose to use a new funeral business if it was built doesn't mean building one is a good idea.

It's also necessary to consider the kind of facility that would be amenable to those new customers. Are you able to buy an existing building, or will you have to start from scratch and create something entirely new? If you are going the new route, make sure you think about the kind of layout families want. If you're building a funeral home, know that many existing ones are just that—homes. Old, dark ones. But that's not what families are looking for today. When they step through the doors, families are inevitably walking into a building they don't want to be in. The last thing they want is for it to meet their worst fears as far as what it looks like. When you're building from the ground up, you can address this preference. Consider creating a larger reception area and dedicating less space to merchandise. Prioritize a light, open interior wherever you can—in the foyer, chapel, and arrangement offices. You want the opposite of customers' associations: nothing dark, cold, or sterile.

Here, size matters too. You have to determine whether the real estate costs too much relative to what you'll get out of it. It's easy to get caught up in the ego boost of having your name on a shiny new sign and advertising that you're a dual-location operator. But there's no sense in building the Taj Mahal if community members are more apt to do a unique service that probably won't involve the cavernous chapel you're imagining. A restaurant business, for instance, could be successful based solely on the fact that it seems busy. Meanwhile, if the owner can't fill the dining room because it's just too big, people will assume that something must be wrong. There's an art to creating the right structure and the corresponding traffic. The funeral profession isn't exempt. You have to think about how you're going to use your facility and make sure that whatever you build serves that purpose.

To determine whether you're spending money just to spend or making an investment that will help you advance your business and meet your goals, conduct a little exercise. Imagine yourself as a shareholder in your company. What would you want the owner to do? How would you want them to operate in order to enhance the value you'll get?

Location, Location, Location

It's not just real estate that counts; location does too. For example, you can have a two-hundred-call funeral home in rural Tennessee that brings in $1 million in sales and a funeral home handling the same number of calls in Phoenix, Arizona, that pulls in just $400,000 per year. What accounts for the difference? Consumer preferences. Cremation rates, the size of the service—if one is held at all—and many other factors all reflect those preferences and have a price tag attached. And they differ from location to location. For example, coastal communities and those with big universities in states like Florida, Hawaii, Oregon, and Washington have markets with much higher cremation rates compared to the rest of the US. It's usually associated with education and the transient nature of the community, and, ironically, wealth. The longer the driveway, the shorter the bill at the funeral home or cemetery—as they say.

People call Johnson Consulting all the time wanting to know the value of their two-hundred-call business. With just the number of calls to go on, we can't possibly give them an answer. Consider those hypothetical funeral businesses located in rural Tennessee and urban Arizona, respectively. The first may have a business value of $1 million, since the community is more attached to tradition and full-body burials, but the real estate the building sits on may be worth just $600,000. In Phoenix, sales may hover at a comparably low $400,000, because so many buyers choose cremation, but the business's real estate may be worth $1 million—another location-based factor that affects business value. So, where do you want to be, if you have the choice? Ideally in small to midsize markets, since the tendency to adhere to tradition in conjunction with real estate value is likely to provide more bang for your buck.

The Napkin Approach

After your market study is complete and you've considered your options when it comes to your facility and its location, it's time to take what I call the napkin approach. It's a way to determine the feasibility for both value and cost. First, let's assume you build the right size building with your customer in mind. We'll say it costs about $1 million to get up and running. Now, if you had to sell it right away, what would it take to justify that million-dollar acquisition?

Let's break that down. We'll assume that the funeral business with the real estate included is worth $1 million. Take that $1 million and divide it by the average market multiple that we typically see when we broker businesses: for this exercise, let's use six times. The business should have $166,666 in EBITDA. Now, we need to use a benchmark of the EBITDA. For most small businesses, that's about 28 percent of net sales. So, we would divide $166,666 by 28 percent and find that sales would need to be about $600,000 to make it worth our while.

But what would the average sale be? Maybe it's $3,500 per funeral before cash advances. That means the business needs to service 171 families on an annual basis to be worth the investment.

This calculation doesn't mean that you should or shouldn't move forward, but it is a napkin-quick way to determine how far off you are. If you're only going to be able to get fifty calls per year, then that million dollars you would borrow or use from your savings would be better off in the stock market or somewhere else.

Cemetery Concerns

Thinking about building or buying a cemetery? These businesses come with their own set of concerns. There is somewhat of a bell curve involved in terms of value. If you're planning to build a new cemetery, you're talking about taking an asset—in this case, a valuable piece of land—and putting a human body in the ground. When you do that, you're getting something with a significant price tag attached to it and making it worthless in terms of real estate value.

You may be able to segment the development to preserve some of that value, determining that you won't develop a portion of the property so that it can serve as absolute collateral for the other loans you might need, like construction. You certainly don't want to use all four corners of a lot only to find yourself unsuccessful with nothing to sell. Instead, you need to think about how to use the land wisely so that if things don't work out, there is still excess property available. This is usually accomplished by first creating a "master plan" of your cemetery, complete with phases of development.

There are also other expenses to think about when you're first setting up, many of which are similar to building a new home. What does that master plan look like? How will you get water lines to your location? How will you maintain it? What about the roads?

Think back to that bell curve. There is a lot of loss on the front end, when you're taking that land, investing in infrastructure, and rendering the areas where you're going to do the burials virtually valueless. You also definitely don't want to purchase a cemetery when it's heading toward the end of its life, since you can't bring in new business for much longer at that point. It's essentially sold out—or soon to be. I would say, though, that one positive impact of cremation is that it is extending the life of cemeteries. Inglewood Park Cemetery in Inglewood, California, provides a great example. In the 1970s and '80s, it seemed to be nearing the end of its life, but today, it's experiencing renewed and great success. I suggest a visit sometime to see just how you can successfully extend the life of a seemingly "full" cemetery.

That middle point, though, at the height of the bell curve, is the sweet spot. Once things are up and running—established and with family heritage, but with room to grow—cemeteries can be extremely valuable, worth more than any other funeral business out there. They're also incredibly hard to come by: it can be difficult to find an owner who would be willing to sell a cemetery right then. And to make matters more interesting, some of the largest operations out there are nonprofit and board-run cemeteries. These cemeteries can be acquired, but with a unique purchase path that differs from the acquisition model of a for-profit cemetery.

If you've owned funeral homes in the past and are thinking about going the cemetery route, know that cemeteries are all about proper development and sales. You're going to have to take that caregiver hat off, put it to the side, and try a sales cap on for size—and that's a struggle for a lot of people. But if you can do it well, it can certainly be worth your while.

Buying—or Creating—a Combo

There's also the notion of combos—those funeral homes located on cemeteries. These businesses can offer a lot of financial promise. For one thing, funeral homes located on cemeteries typically have a higher percentage of burials than those that aren't, since the families choosing these businesses want a one-stop shop. But don't be fooled: simply putting a funeral home on a cemetery doesn't automatically create value. You still have to conduct that market study to make sure the community would be receptive to such a model. In addition, if the business requires construction or development, it's essential to build in such a way that if the funeral home doesn't make it, a buyer could repurpose it as something else. Don't get me wrong, they can be great businesses to own; you just have to develop them wisely—systematically and with a good master plan.

Navigating Your Funding Proposition

You've decided on the right business for your market, including whether you're going to buy or build. The next step is to secure the funding you need, which often requires incurring some debt. Most owners with long-standing businesses don't have much experience in this realm. While it's perfectly fine to have debt on a business—it's the American way—you need to understand how much debt is appropriate, especially if you've been operating with little debt and a lot of extra cash. You're also likely to have built a lifestyle to match, one that may become a little strained if a new business is in your near future.

Why? If there's one thing that's for sure, it's that it takes money to make money. Growth costs money. And if you're going to commit to growth, you need to commit to all the things that come with it, including any necessary financial sacrifices.

Making that commitment isn't for everyone. You have to search deep within yourself and determine whether you're happy with the lifestyle your business provides, or whether you like the idea of growth—and the investment necessary to find greater success in the future. If you want to grow, it's going to be difficult. You're going to have to sacrifice some of the things you've gotten used to—especially if you've had a lifestyle business for a while.

Still interested? Great. Let's talk about what that funding proposition might look like. When you buy an existing funeral home or cemetery business, you'll have the equity or the cash you're going to put in, any loans you'll take on to cover the costs, and one somewhat unique element: a covenant not to compete, or CNC—an amount paid to the previous owner to prevent him or her from competing against you—usually staggered over the course of ten years. While other sectors certainly have CNCs, they're typically much shorter—around six months to two years for a small business in a different industry. Why is the extensive duration necessary? Most people outside our business—bankers included—are totally baffled by the fact that an owner would agree not to compete for such a long time. But it's indicative of the incredible amount of goodwill associated with an owner.

Along with these circumstances are some other challenges specific to funeral businesses. One is securing loans. Let's say you want to buy a funeral business worth $2.4 million, or six times the multiple on cash flow. The real estate is worth half of that—$1.2 million—and the other half is all business value. A bank is always excited to lend on the real estate, because they understand it. It makes sense to them. They'll readily grant you a loan of 75 or 80 percent of the real estate value. It's up to you to come up with the rest. Perhaps that sounds feasible. But what about the other half of the business—the goodwill portion? According to the bank, it has no collateral. There is just no way for them to collateralize it. While there used to be lenders in the space who understood what we do and were willing to lend based on cash flow, knowing that the real estate loan wouldn't cover it all—and simply charged a higher interest rate for taking on that risk—most of them have been gone since the early 2000s. Those cash flow–based lenders are trying to get back in the game, but they aren't there yet. So how do you pay for that business without their help?

Recently, owners have managed this issue by seeking out multiple sources for funding. They get a loan from their bank for the real estate portion, and then another one through the government's SBA program to cover the goodwill. While we can be grateful that the government created such a program, it also means those who go that route will find themselves saddled with paperwork. Lots of it. The application is very long, very detailed, and very black and white. There is one other stipulation that you should know about: there is going to be a lien on just about everything you own. Basically the loan can end up being overcollateralized.

Yet another challenge? You'll be dealing with the full standby provision associated with the SBA. With this provision, the SBA is essentially telling you that they don't know how successful you will be. So, for two years, five years, or even for the entire life of the loan, you're not allowed to pay any other debts associated with the business—the covenant not to compete included. Those stipulations make things pretty difficult if you're trying to bid against other buyers who aren't using an SBA program. Put simply, they can pay the CNC, and you can't. Also, when you consider cemetery acquisition financing, it gets even tougher. It is hard for a bank to want to collateralize land as backing for the loan. Property owners own the land or the rights to interment, not you!

Some banks are willing to help you get around this with fixed debt service charge coverage. In these instances, the bank wants to know that you have around 140 percent, or 1.4 times the amount, of your loan available to ensure they can collect their payments, even during slow months. For example, if you have, say, annually $100,000 principal, plus interest, the bank wants proof that you have $140,000 annually on hand that is produced by the business. For some, as long as your debt coverage ratio is 140 percent, they'll allow you to pay the covenant. Recently, I have seen banks accept this as low as 1.25 times the loan amount. Just be careful, as ratios can be misleading. For example, if the annual free cash available to service the debt is $1,000,000, then at 1.4 times, the bank is happy and will still have a good amount of cash left. However, consider a business with only $120,000 in free cash annually and the debt service ratio happily satisfied at 1.4 times for the bank. While they are happy, I can assure you that you won't be. Why? There won't be very much cash left over. This is why smaller businesses often end up with a lesser valuation multiple.

As you can see, where there's a will, there's a way. You can sort through it all and get the funding you need. But there's a lesson to be learned as well: if you want to start a funeral business in the future—no matter how far out—you need to start working on it *now*. It doesn't matter if you're going to do it tomorrow, a year from now, or five years down the road. It takes time to understand how all of this plays out and to position yourself to buy or build successfully.

Inheriting a Business

If you're inheriting a business, you'll probably avoid some of the loan-related rigmarole. And for that (in addition to the great honor your family is bestowing upon you) you're very fortunate. I was too—my consulting company was a gift from my parents, and it is a true privilege to carry on their legacy. But there are concerns and responsibilities that come with inheriting a business too.

Typically, when you inherit a business, you're also inheriting all of the liability within the corporation, meaning that you are doing a stock transfer and not an asset transfer. What does that look like? Imagine a basket full of eggs. Each of those eggs is an asset you need to run that business. Now, reach into the basket and grab one of the eggs. That first one you pull is real estate, and it has a certain value associated with it. The next one is goodwill. Another egg represents your business's signage. Each one is yours to manage as you see fit, but they are also associated with a particular value. When you purchase the assets of an existing business, you're filling a basket with new eggs typically in what would be called an asset purchase structure. Those values are reflected on your balance sheet at their current market value, and the government allows you to "redepreciate" them, which enables you to save on taxes and grow your operation. This is what an accountant would call a "stepped-up basis" in your assets. But if that business was instead a stock-based purchase, as opposed to an asset purchase, you're taking the basket of assets at their currently depreciated value, which will have negative tax implications for you. Additionally, certain liabilities can transfer with the business, which can add legal risk. You can't put those eggs into a new business and claim that depreciation—it was already used long ago. As such, your taxes will be more. Therefore, you may find that, in this case, it may be better to buy than to receive. When gifted a business or acquiring the stock, you also get the wonderful gem of "depreciation recapture," which essentially means that all of that depreciation benefit that was given by the IRS to the former owner now needs to be paid back to the government when you sell. Lucky you! Not.

Whether it's the right time to build or buy a new facility or simply stick with what you have, staffing is a common—and important—concern. The customer service that staff members provide, and associated sales, is at the crux of our operations. As such, it's essential to get your staffing right so you don't get buried in the process. Let's head there next.

CHAPTER 4

Your Most Valuable Asset: Building a Staff You Can Trust

Staffing is crucial to any organization—funeral or cemetery related or otherwise. We all need to have the right people on board to make our businesses work. But in our profession, staffing comes with its own set of challenges, making it one of the biggest struggles for most owners.

As you certainly know by now, with 110 or fewer funerals per year, most funeral businesses are primarily manned by owners, usually with the help of just one part- or full-time employee. The owner and perhaps a colleague are filling multiple roles: handling administrative tasks, arranging, directing, embalming—soup to nuts. To top it off, they're essentially on call twenty-four hours a day. As these businesses get bigger, tasks become more segmented. A business servicing around four hundred calls might have three or four arrangers, each of them essentially operating their own small business within the business.

Regardless of the size of the organization, when the time does come to look for new staff members, owners are not getting hundreds of applications. These days, technology has made the world and its diversity of options more accessible, showing people the many possibilities out there. With so many opportunities, it's far less appealing to take on a role where you're always on call, the pay can be low, and you're managing grief on a daily basis—along with potentially harmful bodily fluids (after all, when someone is killed in a car accident, you don't necessarily hear about any blood- or airborne pathogens their body may be harboring).

Of course, working in our profession can be incredibly rewarding too. It's a chance to make a difference in the lives of families experiencing loss, something that many find to be a powerful benefit. But it does take a special kind of person to do this work, and many of them are already spoken for. They're working somewhere else in town or in a business out of state. Thus, finding the right people often requires poaching them. And if you're going to lure talent from another owner in your network—one that you probably know pretty well—it's not going to make for a very amicable lunch the next time you have a business association meeting.

This is made all the more challenging by states that require funeral directors to be licensed, limiting the pool even further. And it's unfortunate—especially when you think about the fact that there is a plethora of talented wedding coordinators who could be putting their skills to good use by switching to the funeral business or even supplementing their income by doing arrangements part time alongside their regular slate of nuptials.

Timing may also be an issue. When you reach a point where you've decided to add another staff member to your organization, you may be pretty burned out—having gone weeks or even months without a day off. You want to fill the position, and you want to do it now. But trust me, as appealing as it may seem in the moment, you don't want the first warm body that walks through the door. The employees you have on board affect your business in a big way, especially if there are just a handful of them. As such, it's worth it to hold out and find the right person, even if it means a few more months of doing it all.

Hiring the Right Talent

When you do find a promising candidate, how do you determine that he or she is the right fit for your business? Background checks and any necessary licensing are a nonnegotiable part of the process, of course, but personality also plays a big role. You should think about whether they will be easy to work with. In addition to multiple rounds of interviews with current staff members, you can conduct a DiSC (dominance, influence, steadiness, conscientiousness) profile.[10] These assessments evaluate both personality and behavioral style, particularly within the workplace. The profile will provide additional insight into how that candidate will mesh with you or your team.

If they will be meeting with families, you can also use this information to determine how those interactions will go. What kind of impression will they make? How do they come off over the phone and in person? If they're handling an annual average of fifty to eighty families in your business, we could be talking about hundreds of thousands of dollars in revenue. That's a big responsibility to place on the shoulders of someone who isn't the owner, and who spends all day surrounded by death—a situation most people avoid like the plague. If anything about their personality or behavior serves as a deterrent to potential customers, you may be looking at significant losses. After all, losing just one family could mean giving up as much as $20,000 in enterprise value.

Training for Success

When you find a person who can handle that kind of burden, it's up to you to train them to succeed. You have to ensure they have the skills, tools,

---

10   "DiSC Overview." DiSC Profile. Accessed May 26, 2019. https://www.discprofile.com/what-is-disc/overview/.

and information to meet your expectations—and those of the customer. As such, training should be an ongoing process that continues throughout their time with your organization. You should, however, set the tone from the get-go, and that begins with onboarding.

Onboarding

You may already know that when you start or assume responsibility for a funeral organization, it's pretty much baptism by fire. You're thrown right in and you have to just work through it, hoping that the burns won't be too severe. But it doesn't have to be that way for your employees. You can figure out how to extinguish those fires and create a clear path in their place. And you do that by creating a strategic plan with long-term goals, one that will dictate your company's direction, key initiatives, and culture—all of which should be communicated during your onboarding process.

In other businesses, HR might handle these kinds of initiatives, but for many of us, that's not a function we have the luxury of depending on. It's up to the owner or office manager to oversee any HR-related issues, or it's outsourced to a payroll company. That means it's on you to share your vision and goals with the staff as they join your organization.

Then, you have to make sure that information sticks. Within the first thirty days, you should sit down with a recent hire and see how things are going. Do they need more training or clarity on any aspect of their role or the business as a whole? The same process should happen again at the sixty- and ninety-day marks. It's important to stay in touch with staff members as they move forward, particularly in a very small workplace setting. Why? When you're likely talking about a culture among three or four people, bringing one person on who isn't familiar with or amenable to it could be deadly.

Don't just stop after those ninety days are up, even if things are going smoothly. You have to continue to identify and address gaps in knowledge and experience and keep employees involved in the strategic plan, updating them as it evolves.

Creating Cadence

One way to keep purpose—and productivity—alive is to create a meeting cadence within your business. You're not meeting just to meet, but to develop rhythm and a pattern of communication, one where employees can expect meetings to start and end on time and rest assured that they will be informed of any necessary developments. This, in turn, helps them live up to their expectations.

Regular morning huddle meetings to discuss the day's activities are of course important, but you should also make time to meet on a weekly basis to talk about where you are in relation to your goals—including average sales and case counts—as well as other happenings that are occurring within the organization. I use a flash report on a weekly basis that monitors the number of calls my funeral business has and the overall average sales associated with them. I then compare that to my budgeted calls and revenue and create transparency by sharing that information with my staff. Quarterly meetings provide an opportunity to review your strategic plan and benchmark your progress as well.

If they feel like their work is worthwhile and they are contributing to something bigger than themselves, they will be more motivated to succeed.

People want to know how they fit into the organization. They want to know that they make a difference. It's a factor that matters just as much as compensation. If they feel like their work is worthwhile and they are contributing to something bigger than themselves, they will be more motivated to succeed. And if you're not meeting on a regular basis, your team isn't getting any of that motivation.

They're just doing their job day in and day out, and that's not a way to live, especially in an environment that is so focused on death. The key is to make sure they understand their own purpose in addition to yours, and keeping them in the loop can help make that happen.

Compensation and Incentive Plans

As you create your approach to training, it may be worthwhile to think about compensation and incentive plans. Why? Whatever you incent someone to do, they will do—for better or for worse. If you want to create behaviors that align with your purpose and direction, then an incentive plan is one way to do it. Of course, you first have to start with your strategic plan, develop that purpose and direction to begin with, and ensure that anyone and everyone in your business knows it. But an incentive plan can help drive it home. Let's look at how these types of plans may play out.

As an owner, a certain portion of your revenue is allocated toward payroll expenses. In an ideal world, those expenses should be around 30 to 35 percent of net sales, owner compensation not included. They should, however, include general compensation, insurance costs, taxes, 401(k) plans, bonuses, uniforms—anything related to labor within your organization.

If you've had a particularly good year, hitting all of your performance targets, you may want to provide the employees who helped you achieve those results with bonuses to recognize a job well done. Often, those bonuses comprise a percentage of their pay—no less than 5 percent and no more than around 25 percent. Then, you have to figure out how to pay it. Will everyone receive the same 5 percent bonus at the end of the year, or will it be based on individual performance? If the goal is to drive home each employee's role in achieving business goals, you may want to go with the latter option.

When we create a compensation plan at Johnson Consulting, we typically look at these main three areas, among others (depending on the goals of the business):

- Average sale: What is the average sale made by any employees who meet with families, such as arrangers? The goal isn't to turn anyone into a salesperson, but you do want to hold them accountable. Staff members should be taking the families on a tour of all of the products and services available to them. If they don't, they're doing the family—and your business—a disservice. We use our JCG Performance Tracker software (JCGPerformanceTracker.com) to monitor the behavior of thousands of funeral professionals. With a quick scan of the data stored in our tracker, it's easy to identify the employees that take families on a good tour of all the offerings and those who don't.

- Collections: Your staff members may be great at making presentations and showing families the value of the various products and services available to them, but if they don't collect any money, they've just wasted a couple of hours of everyone's day. As we established, there's not much recourse if a family doesn't pay. Services have been rendered, and there's really no going back. To determine how good staff members are at collecting money, divide the annual sales for a year by the company's average amount of accounts receivable. Is the money coming through relatively quickly, or are things dragging? At a funeral home, ten to fifteen days is on the low end, while forty-five days or more may indicate an issue with collections.

- Customer service: Say your arranger has done a thorough presentation and collected the money. If the family didn't like how they did either or both of those things—if they sounded too much like a salesperson or took on a tone that wasn't appreciated—then the customer service they provided wasn't up to par (more on how to gauge their performance on this crucial aspect in just a moment).

For each of those measures, designate a percentage of the dollar amount they could receive, based on its importance to you. Did they have personal goals for each area, and did they hit them? Did you see improvements based on your professional development efforts? From there, you can determine their overall performance score rating and their corresponding bonus.

You can also create an incentive program where the funds are distributed based on their ongoing performance. Consider choosing a quarterly timeframe over a monthly one, which provides a bit more time for their efforts to level out. Any additional compensation would be based on those three factors mentioned above. How are their average sales compared to the operation's sales expectations? Are their receivables under a certain number of days? What do their customer service metrics look like? Once that quarter is over, simply plop those scores into your formula and—ta-da!— you've just designated how much that employee is going to get. That way, too, when you let them know the amount they will be receiving, you can also show them everything that went into it. It becomes very obvious there is no owner discretion involved.

Then again, a little discretion isn't always a bad idea. You could withhold a portion of the funds to be used as a discretionary bonus at the end of the year and proceed with a formula based on quarterly achievement. That gives you the opportunity to give a bit more when all is said and done if they didn't hit goals but worked hard, or if you simply want to recognize their loyalty. It's one of the perks of being an owner: we get to do whatever we want.

It's nice to be human about it, though, no matter how many formulas you use. If your employees have put in the effort, there should be room to offer money for hard work and improvements made—even if they haven't quite hit their targets. You just don't want to make a habit out of it. If you do, you're defeating the purpose of an incentive plan.

Customer Service

Since customer service is a key expectation for many staff members, let's take a deeper dive into this crucial area next. In his book *The Customer Service Revolution*, John DiJulius explains the reality that everything inevitably becomes a commodity, including the services we provide. Especially with software and other online applications, people are looking for simple, easy, quick. As such, one of the most valuable ways to differentiate your business is through customer service.

As you know, there are real consequences if your customer service isn't the best it can be: every customer counts. Significant enterprise value is lost with just one disgruntled family. Moreover, you'll be lucky if they don't share their disappointing experience with others, killing additional sales in the process.

And lest we forget, the customer isn't the dead person; it's the family. You have to determine how to make an impact on those around to experience it. If you ask funeral home owners and cemeterians what sets them apart, they'll often mention their customer service. But the funny part is, the family already expects high-quality customer service. You may be proud of what you've done, but most likely, you haven't under- or overwhelmed them; they've just been whelmed, as Chip and Dan Heath describe in their book *The Power of Moments*.

Maybe you checked off the boxes on your list, hitting what you consider to be the high notes, but if those gestures weren't particularly meaningful to the family, you're not going to have the kind of impact that will help set you apart. Those whelming experiences are not what people remember. It's the peak moments that stick out.

So how do you transform the customer experience within your organization into the stuff of peak moments? It can be hard to know. As a funeral professional, there probably isn't a lot of competition in your community to use for comparison. At Johnson Consulting Group, we have constructed a customer-service program to integrate and keep customer service as a number-one priority within the business … and it works! I have used the same program at my own funeral business.

Good customer service begins with knowing not only what your customers expect but also what they want. To figure that out, you have to ask. It's easy to get bogged down with all of the details and forget to ask the family what is really important to them. But that question is necessary to go above and beyond.

The next thing you need to get is feedback. This usually comes in the form of a survey after the service, burial, or cremation is complete. I don't mean to be grim, but many funeral business owners miss the mark here—and you might be one of them. Those who do conduct surveys often go for the feel-good stuff. I see this all the time in the businesses I work with, and in some ways, it's a logical move: it's easier to lean on easy questions that don't bruise the ego. Instead of asking, "What could we have done to make your experience better?" funeral professionals ask customers to rate the experience on a scale of 1–5 or to name the person who stood out most during the experience. Those questions are important, but they don't provide all the feedback needed. You need to get to the heart of the matter, even if it requires facing some uncomfortable truths.

Good customer service begins with knowing not only what your customers expect but also what they want.

In this situation, getting an outside perspective can be very helpful. Many premier firms use Johnson Consulting to help with surveying their customers. We conduct well over one hundred thousand surveys for funeral businesses across the country each year, using the JCG Performance Tracker web application software that works in a methodical and process-driven manner, with actuarial formulas designed to understand just how good a customer's experience was and how likely they are to return. It's a full two-page survey, and the feedback that comes through is far better than the fluff that comes back from a few surface-level questions.

When you have enough data, even the smallest subtleties between one employee and another become visible, and customer service is no exception. Issuing thorough surveys that don't shy away from the tough stuff helps owners get a clear picture of how their staff members are performing when it comes to customer service—and how they can improve. With higher-quality feedback, you and your staff can modify the experience where it counts, creating peak moments and staying away from just "whelming" the family.

Succession

You've hired the right person and trained them to believe in your purpose and embody your culture while creating a meaningful experience for your customer. Their performance is excellent, but what happens when they want to take on more responsibility? Succession poses a real issue in our business, particularly with our notoriously short corporate ladders. Maybe an employee starts working part time, answering phones and filling out paperwork, and eventually becomes the office manager. Or someone begins on the funeral-directing side, and soon takes on arrangements as well. They pursue a license in embalming next, with the idea that one day they may manage the whole operation or even become an owner.

While efforts like these are very admirable, employees can quickly find themselves stuck within an organization. They may be a key arranger, but that's as far as they can go, because the only person with more responsibility is the owner. If that's the case, the options are to enjoy the role within the organization, find a bigger funeral or cemetery business, or consider starting a business on their own, which can be difficult (flip back to the previous chapter for a quick refresher on why, if you'd like).

Larger funeral homes or cemeteries usually offer longer ladders with more rungs but, as discussed, staff members (and their managers) often find that the traits that make someone exceptional at one position don't necessarily translate to another. Moreover, the higher you go, the humbler you need to be, and the more you need to empower those underneath you, with as little ego as possible. Those who can't let go of their own perceived self-importance can snuff out their careers or even the organization at large—all while angering and alienating their colleagues.

But maybe you as the owner are ready to let go of some of your responsibility. You want to prepare that key staff member to fill your shoes someday. You're training your number two in each area of your business, and they've taken on every new role with gusto. Before you hand over the keys and book a trip to somewhere warm, pause.

You know that much of your business value consists of goodwill. If the families in your community begin to identify your number two as the owner before you're ready to sell, they may start to obtain the upper hand. You don't want to put yourself in that dreaded situation, where you want to sell them the business and they won't meet your price because they already have so much equity value in the form of relationships.

To manage this situation, you have to build a solid plan. By all means, train that exceptional employee to take over some of the grunt work and develop their skills, so if the day does come for them to take over the business, they are equipped to do so. But make sure you're not accidentally giving your organization away in the process. You have to engage in mushroom management—keeping them safely under your cap—so they don't end up owning the business before you sell it to them.

With a trusted team on hand to help you meet your goals, it's time to look at two concepts that many funeral business owners don't consider, despite their inherent value: growth and innovation. If you're interested in building something that's greater than the lifestyle itself—or simply staying afloat as your community's interests inevitably change—the next chapter is a must-read.

CHAPTER 5

Going beyond the Grave: Finding Growth and Innovation in the Funeral and Cemetery Businesses

Let's kick off our discussion on growth and innovation with a simple question: *Why do people choose you?*

Many funeral home owners would say people choose them because they've served those families before and they do a good job. Cemeterians typically respond similarly. And for them, there's an added bonus when it comes to choice: if other family members are already buried there, chances are they're going to come back.

These answers may indeed be valid. But if you've read this far, you know that the reasons people buy are changing across virtually every industry. Price, access, and simplicity all matter more than ever before to consumers, whether they are looking to get a new pair of pants or a mortgage. While some of us may not have seen them yet, those changes are coming for us too. And if you have any desire to grow—or even just keep the business you have—it's time to get innovative.

A Fixed Death Rate Doesn't Prohibit Growth

In this business, many of us have embraced the idea that growth can be tough, if not impossible. We tell ourselves we're in a relatively fixed market—that there are only so many deaths per year (though flu season can be a real killer), and our organizations service a set percentage of those deaths. With the knowledge that there's not much we can do to influence the death rate—nothing legal, anyway—bringing in more business is not a common topic of conversation among funeral and cemetery business owners.

So, when asked why people choose them, most funeral and cemetery business owners are not singing the praises of the things that attract people today. They're not touting exceptional marketing practices or great prices or the fact that they've capitalized on convenience—ingratiating customers with the ease of buying they provide. The fact is, many of us have never had to worry about those things, and so we haven't. As such, we haven't invested time, energy, or money in the things that matter to customers today. But we've got to change our tune.

This doesn't have to be bad news, though. Quite the contrary. It's a great opportunity. And you may find that seeking out growth—and the innovation necessary to achieve it—is not just good for business; it's good for you, too, giving you the chance to get creative and find more fulfillment in your work. It just takes a little homework. And the first step is figuring out your buyer persona.

Know Your Buyer Persona

You may have heard the term "buyer persona" before. It refers to the kind of person who typically uses a particular product or service. Other markets think about them all the time—they're considering the type of person who shops for the stuff they offer and adjusting accordingly. Most funeral business owners haven't considered who their typical buyers are, though. Some may even argue that their usual customers don't do much talking. But it's crucial to remember that our customers are the families we're serving, not the people who have passed. Therefore, just like any other business, there tends to be a type of individual who comes to us based on where we're located and what we offer. Knowing your buyer persona—and your market—allows you to think about your customers' goals and interests, so that you can better cater to their needs.

Of course, while other markets may be looking for repeat buyers—for instance, a restaurant owner hopes their customers will return once or even twice a week, basing their buyer persona on who's likely to show up the most—things aren't quite the same for us. Our buyers rarely visit more than once or twice in a lifetime. But if you know your market and the kind of person who's coming to you, it doesn't matter that they don't visit very often. You can still deliver an experience a lot like the one they get with other products and services they access: quick, transparent, and right on target.

How do you pinpoint your buyer persona? Start by thinking about your market. Are you in a highly traditional one, one like my old hometown of Batesville, Indiana, where funerals are community affairs—complete with visitations, services, and full-body burials? Or are you serving an area where people are pretty transient? Perhaps you're somewhere warm, sunny, and full of retirees, where cremation rates are skyrocketing. Is there a strong religious segment in your area, and are you serving that population, or do they head to another business that's more aligned with their traditions? Once you determine the environment you're in, you can hone in on your typical customer.

If you're in a traditional market, maybe your buyer persona is Glenda Smith, a seventy-five-year-old woman who's lived in your town all her life and just lost her husband of fifty years. She wouldn't dream of doing anything less than her friends and neighbors do. And that means she'll want a complete package, with a visitation, formal funeral service, and limo rides to the cemetery, where her husband will be buried with the rest of the Smiths in a coveted spot overlooking the nearby rose garden.

Or maybe you're in a market where cremation is the norm. It's a place that no one's really from; people just come to escape the winters, spending six months of the year playing tennis, having lunch at "the club," and hosting their grandchildren. There, your buyer persona might be the family of Tom Brown. They live two thousand miles away, and they're over-whelmed by the logistics of it all. With a network spread out across the country and just a few close friends in your community, there aren't enough people who would come to the service to make having one worth their while. The family is certain they want to keep things as simple as possible. It will be cremation for them, and most everyone else who lives there.

Or perhaps you're somewhere in between, where full-body burials still happen on a regular basis, but cremation rates are picking up speed.

No matter the circumstances, when you know your market and your buyer, you can adapt, changing your marketing and presentation messaging along with your delivery to fit their needs. Keep in mind that you can have more than one buyer persona at your business. Understanding each persona helps you know how and where you should be marketing along with what your internal speak and messaging is with those different families. When you do, you'll set yourself apart from your competitors and bring in more traffic. But you may have to address your own mind-set first.

Be Adaptable

Attitudes are changing. People's feelings about tradition have shifted, and cremation, nonchurch funerals, home funerals, body donations, and green funerals are all growing in popularity and occupying a place in the market.

People also want personalization. Most customers like to think of themselves as snowflakes with unique traits. You have to make sure the options you offer speak to their interests. (Remember buyer personas!) This can be a challenge, especially if you've been doing things the same way for generations. But if you decide you're just going to turn a blind eye to those who want something different, begrudging them for not understanding the value of tradition and memorialization and declaring that if they don't want you, you don't want them either, you're going to end up losing a lot of business—especially down the line. Adjusting your offerings doesn't mean overlooking the people who do want to go the traditional route; you have to have everything in place for them too. But it can require a shift in perspective and the willingness to branch out into less familiar territory.

Whether or not you feel your customer is in denial of dying, whether or not you agree with their grieving process just doesn't matter. You can fight it, or you can embrace it. If you can't meet their needs, they're going to go elsewhere. By the same token, when people know you can solve their problem in a manner that suits their needs and interests, you'll be the one they call. Taking that tack is the route to growth.

We all handle death differently, and sometimes in quite radical ways. Funeral arrangers have a juggling act on their hands every time they answer the phone or meet with a family. If you're on the front lines, at the core, you're solving that problem, but you're also battling with families' grief, their perception of you, and the five million different things running through their heads. How can your business address that problem while assuaging that

... when people know you can solve their problem in a manner that suits their needs and interests, you'll be the one they call.

family's fears, offering comfort, and providing options that make them feel seen and heard?

First, take a look at your display room. Is it mostly devoted to caskets and full-body burial options, or are there plenty of cremation and memorialization choices present—including less traditional items like keepsakes and jewelry? These are all opportunities to add to the family's experience and—quite frankly—to your own revenue. Let's face it: this is a business. And the products and services you offer should reflect that. You can also evaluate your services. For instance, if a family is choosing to have a funeral somewhere other than your facility—like at their own home—are you remaining involved and offering them other opportunities for memorialization, or are you letting them walk out the door to take it from there on their own? All of these factors have an impact on value. To understand just how much, start by looking at trends in your call volume.

Monitor Value

Say you're a 500-call firm. If, five years ago, you were a 675-call firm, your current valuation is going to be different than one for a 500-call firm that was doing 300 calls five years ago and from one that has maintained a steady 500-call rate over time. If you were doing 675 calls a handful of years ago and now you're down to 500, you're probably not a high-value 500-call firm. But if you were doing 300 calls before and now you're up to 500, things are really looking up. And if you have been doing 500 calls for years on end, you're likely the most valuable of all. Why? Each of those years, you were handling 500 different deaths. Customers have continued to come to you, whether they're returning for another loved one or they're finding you for the first time, and that means whatever you're doing is working. But there's always room to do more, and to increase your cash flow in the process.

For example, let's say you've been a 500-call firm for years. When you look into your offerings and compare them to other businesses in your area, you see that there is more you could be doing. You decide to institute some additional service options and training with your arrangers and add about $100 more to your average sale as a result. Over the course of a year, your revenue grows by $50,000, since that additional value was all in service. That's quite a boon. But it doesn't stop there. In addition to that revenue, every dollar in this case roughly translates to $6 in enterprise value. If you find a way to save $1,000, you've just earned yourself $6,000 in enterprise value. Thus, if your revenue has grown by $50,000 and your firm is trading at six times EBITDA, you've increased your enterprise value by $300,000. That's great news!

But there's bad news too. The same rationale holds true for losses. If you lose $100 per sale because you're not adapting to all the changes in the market, it might not sound like much money, but it's actually quite a lot. Let's say you're losing an average of $150 per sale in a 500-call firm. That would be $450,000 in lost value overall.

A lot of firms don't think about it this way; to them, the numbers seem somewhat arbitrary. But believe me, when it's time to sell, it gets very real. Let's say Johnson Consulting is helping to sell your business. We've determined that your business's current average sale is $4,500, when two years ago it was $4,700. That means you can kiss a whopping $600,000 in enterprise value goodbye.

Thankfully, there's more good news. If you can understand what your average sale is, you can do something about it and boost your value in the process. For example, many cemeterians may find themselves losing families due to the cremation rate. Rather than burying their loved ones like they used to, they're having them cremated and taking them home. One way to deal with that is to make sure the product options you offer related to cremation are known—or add more to the list if you don't provide them already. From interment to columbariums, scattering, and ossuaries, even private estates with a full family headstone and a vault of urns, there are so many routes a family can take. But if you don't share the options available or you don't know what's missing—what your customer might want or need—you're pretty much stuck.

You don't have to be, though. Simply speak up. Tell customers about what you offer, ask them what they want, and try to make it happen if you're not doing so already. The next step is to communicate with local funeral homes to let them know about your offerings, since they see your customers first and can help spread the word.

Of course, strategy matters too. Options are definitely important, but as cemeterians and funeral home owners, we can't just take the Baskin-Robbins approach of offering thirty-one flavors. Whenever you're considering a new product, you have to weigh how much of a value it will be to the customer. Software companies, for instance, employ a scoring system. They determine the products they'll develop based on the estimated value they'll provide to the customer and to the company. You can—and should—take the same approach.

Without buyers who return frequently, you don't have the same luxury a restaurant owner might have, comparing orders week after week. But there are ways to harness the metrics you do have. Implementing the right accounting systems and surveys that ask the tough questions are good places to start. They can give you a read on whether anything new you're instituting is making a difference, for better or for worse.

We all have some downtime here and there, when we end up with all kinds of ideas. But it would be a far better use of your time to develop a strategic plan and make sure anything new you're dreaming up aligns with your overall approach. If you've gotten a business valuation and you've been monitoring various metrics to see how different factors are affecting overall value, you can determine whether that seemingly great idea is really worth your time. Eventually, you can develop a matrix so when something new occurs to you, you can run it through your system before trying to implement it (and potentially save yourself some money in the process).

You should be monitoring value just like you monitor cash in the bank or keep an eye on your stock portfolio. Your business won't grow through osmosis. It's not going to just work out in the end because you hope it will. You have to have a strategy to make sure whatever you're doing is good for the customer and creates value for you too. It all goes back to starting with the end in mind. But before you can get into the weeds with value and what your customer wants, you have to show up in the community. Otherwise, you're pretty much dead to them.

Build a Community Presence

One of the most important tactics in cultivating growth may seem relatively old school, especially in the presence of so much talk on change, but it remains essential. No matter what your neck of the woods looks like, you have to build a community presence. Owners and staff alike have to be out there, showing the neighbors that they're here to stay—even if the neighbors themselves tend to move around. Make your name known within local religious associations. Get involved in the hospice organizations nearby. Engage in philanthropic efforts that show people you care.

> *When something as difficult and personal as death happens, customers go with who they trust and know.*

Why is community presence so important in this day and age, when most people spend more time staring at their screens than connecting in person? When something as difficult and personal as death happens, customers go with whom they trust and know.

That's a big deal, and it can be a tough thing to remember. Even the best entrepreneurs can be guilty of working so much on the construction and delivery of their services, on identifying those buyer personas, on building strategy and meeting with their staff, that they forget to get out of their office and into the community. They forget to make themselves known, be that resource, and give back. But doing that is essential to overall success.

Since the very beginning of the funeral and cemetery service professions, developing mayoral and heritage status has been key for our business operators. Technology is certainly changing things, but as you well know by now, it's slow going, and there's no substitute for a familiar face. Building a successful plan for growth actually begins with getting back to your roots and practicing the fundamentals of what funeral businesses have been known for: being community fixtures, ones people can count on in the saddest of circumstances. When you do that, you can begin to take things further.

Put It All Out There

While there's no substitute for getting out there in person, you have to build a web presence too—something we'll cover in detail in the next chapter. After all, you have to think about any and every way a customer might find you. And just as they look for household cleaning products, vacations, and even dates online, they now look for funeral businesses that way too.

Most of our markets aren't too crowded with other competitors, and that means you're likely to show up toward the top of the list when they search. That's great, but it doesn't mean your work is done when you sign up for a website. Making it attractive and easy to navigate is important, too, but today, that's all expected. The real differentiators, as far as customers can tell, are price and online reviews. Whether they've been introduced to you through a potluck dinner at the local Lions Club or the landing page of your website, pricing and reviews make a significant impact. And that means you may have to post your prices. If you don't, they'll definitely notice. The list of options may be short, but if the second business they see has prices on their website, you may just lose out.

Putting together a list of packages for the website—and your office—is crucial too. You want to make the decision as easy as possible for families. And with the way the rest of the world operates, they're going to count on it. If they have to sift through a general price list and choose the products and services they want one by one, they're not doing that. Most people are looking for simple solutions—a clear path to get everything they need. When it comes to your customer's definition of a "simple" arrangement, though, you'll find that it's a relative term. While one family might envision a simple funeral as a visitation, complete funeral service, a bunch of limousines and a coach, followed by a banquet that can feed every guest, another might see simple as cremation and then picking up their loved one's ashes to take home. You want to make sure you're able to serve as many people as you can, that you don't put yourself in a corner with a package that doesn't leave room for families' wishes. When you have the kinds of services they want and your message is clear, you can get a little creative, making sure you're harnessing every marketing opportunity you have.

Think Outside the Box—or Casket

One interesting way to get people through your doors and show them what you're all about? Pet services. Pet services provide a unique opportunity to increase business—especially if there's not another pet provider in your market—and it's one more funeral service professionals are taking advantage of or considering. Though adding this service can create some additional profit, to me it's more about the marketing. It may sound strange, but offering pet burial or cremation means more families that haven't used your business before are walking through your doors (and perhaps more frequently, since most pets have relatively short life spans). If just one family decides to choose you for one of their human family members, that could be an additional $20,000 in enterprise value. Sounds like a worthwhile endeavor to me.

When it comes to putting it all out there, don't forget the business you're already doing. Every time there's a funeral service on your premises, you have the chance to make an impact—not just on the family who has experienced a loss, but also on all of the people in attendance. From a marketing perspective, that's a great opportunity; it's not every day that you get to truly show people what you can do. If you're on your A game and able to give them a meaningful experience, they're more likely to give you a call when they lose someone close. Are you finding a way to capture their information (respectfully, of course) and provide them with yours? If you're not, you should be.

Today, we have the unique challenge of straddling innovation and tradition at the same time: we can't discount our traditional customers and their long-standing needs and preferences, but at the same time, preferences are changing, and if we don't stay abreast of those changes, we're going to get left behind.

Technology is a big part of that equation too. Right now, we're still serving generations that haven't grown up digitally native, ones who don't necessarily have a Facebook account and may still prefer phone calls to texts, but that won't be true forever. Some of us are dreading that reality; they may even be scared to death. But there's no reason to fear. Today's tech-heavy world is yet another opportunity, as long as you're willing to do the work. Let's talk about what building a tech-savvy funeral business might entail.

CHAPTER 6

What Doesn't Kill You Makes You Stronger: Embracing Technology in a Slow-to-Change Profession

Technology. Whether you love it or hate it, it's impossible to deny that it's infiltrated virtually every part of our lives. You may have adapted readily, relishing the fact that everything you can think of can be delivered straight to your door with the click of a mouse and using FaceTime or Skype to get closer to loved ones who live far away. Perhaps you use it begrudgingly, owning a cell phone but refusing to text. Either way, it's time to recognize that tech is not going anywhere, and our businesses aren't exempt from its presence. It's not just here to stay but here to grow.

The good news is you're not too late to the party—at least in our profession. Funeral home owners and cemeterians aren't typically known for being trendsetters, and we haven't exactly broken the mold with our willingness to embrace technology. But changes are happening, with discount operations popping up in many markets—and posting their prices online—and customers choosing differently and considering online reviews through popular services like Yelp. You can't count on legacy alone anymore.

However, you don't have to be haunted by the prevalence of technology; it's not nearly as scary as you think. And it opens up a whole realm of opportunities, including options to manage your business, connect to and follow up with customers, and even increase sales. If you take the time to get up to speed, you'll see that technology and the many tools it offers are definitely worth your while. Let's start with a tool that can make a major difference in the way you run your office: point-of-sale systems.

Point-of-Sale Systems

You may be familiar with this form of technology already. There are a number of point-of-sale systems (sometimes referred to as case management systems) out there that specifically target our business, systems like FDMS, SRS, HMIS, The Smart Director, CRäKN, and Passare. Many of us use them for project and product management, and they certainly fulfill that purpose. But they can be used for so much more. When you tap into their capabilities, any of these systems helps you manage everyday operations and cultivate ongoing connectivity with the customer, even allowing you to find customers in the first place—all while decreasing your workload.

For instance, consider your day-to-day operations. You likely have a whiteboard in the back of your business with all of the day's activities on it, designating who will handle what. At the end of the day, you or your staff probably clean it up and put up the next day's affairs. More and more point-of-sale systems are incorporating this whiteboard application, allowing you to refine what your staff is doing each day, and make efforts like these much easier. When scheduling and other mundane tasks are automated, your team can focus on the areas where they are most skilled—ones that require a human touch.

Moreover, up until now, few of us realized just how useful these systems could be for CRM—customer relationship management. But today, the companies crafting the systems themselves are beginning to address this opportunity directly, building in features that create the kind of connectivity you or your team may manage personally. For example, some offer online family collaboration centers, where families can communicate details about the funeral and share any necessary information. Without that task on your plate, you can get back to cultivating growth.

If you already have a point-of-sale system in place, check out all the features it comes with and think about how you could use the existing software to do more. If you have a lot on your plate and you don't use this technology yet, now may be a good time to invest. With your internal technology in line, you can turn your attention to the stuff customers see—starting with your website.

Websites

Today, websites are almost a foregone conclusion. As consumers, we assume that every business—large and small—has one. Sharing information online limits suspicion and frustrations alike. This is no different for funeral and cemetery businesses: buyers need to be able to see where you are, how to reach you, and what you offer. Your website should share with potential customers all of the data they need to make a decision, as well as the tools they need to reach you: general information about your business, contact forms for preneed follow-up and lead management, and details on pricing and packages. Remember, if your website doesn't fulfill those basic requirements, customers who haven't dealt with you before are likely heading elsewhere.

For funeral homes, there is another website feature that should be mandatory: obituary listings. Statistics show that for funeral home sites, most traffic comes from people following an obituary (potentially one posted on social media, but more on that in a minute). If you're not currently sharing obituaries online, you should be.

There's another great website-based option for any funeral business owner interested in bringing in more money (hint: that should be all of us): flower sales.

Flower and Merchandise Sales

The flower sales portion of websites has become a phenomenon in and of itself, one that reflects the transient nature of today's society. Nowadays, there are a lot of people who aren't able to make it to the funeral. Most of us just don't live as close to our communities as we used to. But they still want to participate in some way, and it's usually by donating to a charity or sending flowers. Flowers remain a popular choice because people want something there at the funeral that symbolizes their presence. When they live out of town, they rely on the family or the funeral business itself to find out where to purchase flowers. Websites with this function save people the effort. They can go directly to the site, read the obituary, offer their condolences in the comments section, and order their flowers on the spot.

And it's big business. Companies that host funeral business websites are doing very well with their "memorialization center" pages, areas of the site where they sell miscellaneous merchandise in addition to flowers. The companies who own those portals take a cut of what you make, obviously, but you get to share that income. It's been so lucrative that CFS, a business that specializes in creating funeral home websites, offers websites for free as long as you use their flower sale program. If you're looking for an easy way to add value to your business, flower sales are probably for you. Without much effort, you could end up making some good money.

Once your website is up and running, with all the necessary features, you can turn your attention to an area that can be challenging in our profession: social media.

How to Use Social Media

If you've ever wondered about the place of social media in our market, you're not alone. After all, in a culture that avoids death every chance it gets, there aren't many people who want regular updates from the local funeral home or cemetery on their feeds. But that doesn't mean building a social media presence isn't important, or that it doesn't have a place in our sector.

At its core, social media allows you to notify your network about what's going on in your life, and death is no exception. People use the platforms to share not only the happy news—their latest vacation photos or the birth of a child—but the sad stuff too. That makes these channels an appropriate place to post obituaries or the details of a funeral or memorial service. The benefits of putting obituaries and funeral information on social media are twofold: it gives the family a way to notify their community of any updates and provides you with the chance to get the name of your business out there.

That said, you do have to be conscientious about what you post. While obituaries and funeral information have their place on people's feeds, there's a good chance customers and their communities are not terribly interested in a detailed rundown of your everyday operations. And unlike other businesses, your messaging certainly won't be something like "Casket Sale—One Day Only!" Still, the point of social media is engagement, and finding the message that's meaningful to users is important. Here, it's not about self-promotion—I guarantee your potential customer isn't going to be nearly as excited as you are that you've increased your case calls—it's about building brand recognition. That way, when they finally have to reach out, your name is top of mind.

What kinds of messages would be appealing or interesting to the general population? Perhaps you're doing some philanthropic work in the community. That's valuable news to share. Social media platforms are also great for publicizing any events you might be hosting. For instance, as a cemetery, you may have a gathering around the holidays, a ceremony for Easter, or a service in honor of veterans. All are worthy of announcing on your page.

Social media, with its focus on community, is one place to spread the word, but what about another omnipresent form of technological communication: our phones? That's something you can use too.

Texting Programs

Privacy settings notwithstanding, we have the power to know where just about every person in the United States is at any given time. There are companies that have exploited this truth in great ways. Uber, which uses mobile GPS technology to get you from here to there, and Waze, which taps into mobile users' data to identify traffic patterns and provide real-time travel insights, are two great apps thriving thanks to the power of mobile technology. Believe it or not, there's a place for funeral homes and cemeteries to innovate in the mobile space too.

There are businesses in our profession that are utilizing texting to help families notify their contacts of funeral details. This is a simple way to create more simplicity and value for customers. It also provides a lot of good exposure for your business, since your name is being shared with so many individuals, and it's stored right there in their phones. Geolocating a grave at a cemetery or notifications on grief support are a few options.

Crowdfunding

There is yet another avenue for communication that you may not be considering—one that can also increase sales. Maybe you're familiar with crowdfunding, raising funds using an online platform. Facebook and sites like GoFundMe provide people with the opportunity to ask their communities to help them raise money for a cause they care about. When tragedy strikes, people use these platforms as well, asking for support in sad or desperate times.

Tragic situations are ideally suited for significant memorialization, as it gives the community more of an opportunity to get some closure. But more memorialization means more money, and especially if a death has occurred suddenly, families may not have much set aside to cover the cost. That makes crowdfunding the logical answer and a natural fit for the funeral business.

We're kidding ourselves if we believe cost doesn't factor into the decisions we make about how we memorialize our loved ones. I often wonder how much some families would spend on a funeral if money were no option. With crowdfunding, families have an avenue to gain support and thus spend more than they might have been able to otherwise.

This arena does come with its own set of challenges; unfortunately, fraud and poor spending choices can factor in. Families are so overwhelmed by the amount of money coming in that they don't always behave prudently. When possible, we should find ways to be a co-steward of funeral-related crowdfunding initiatives; that way we have the ability to ensure not only that families can honor their loved ones properly but also that the community's contributions are spent in the way that those donors intended—all while potentially increasing our own revenues.

Technology will continue to evolve, modernizing our profession while making our jobs easier—if we're willing to get on board. For example, it will be a magical day when customers can pick their burial space online, without having to make a trip to the cemetery. And it's a day that will most definitely arrive, whether it's sooner or later. Speaking of which, the cemetery sector has its own slate of concerns and advantages in today's market. Next, we'll talk about the issues and opportunities that apply to that space in particular.

CHAPTER 7

From Now till Eternity: Managing a Property Meant to Be Forever

While there are around nineteen thousand funeral homes in the US, there are tens of thousands more cemeteries.[11] Why? Like diamonds, cemeteries are forever. Once you start one, it's never going away. You've put those bodies in the ground, and thus a bank or restaurant or retail store is no longer in that real estate's future. This is a unique proposition, and as such, there are a number of insights that apply to cemeteries alone. Whether you're thinking about starting or buying a cemetery business or you're already in the space, this chapter is for you. We'll begin with the foundation of any good cemetery: building a master plan.

Building a Cemetery Strategy

As a cemeterian, you have a big responsibility: caring for an eternal resting place. And while families only see the surface—the beautiful landscaping and clean, well-cared-for monuments—you're primarily in charge of a

---

11   "Statistics." National Funeral Directors Association. Accessed March 25, 2019.
      http://www.nfda.org/news/statistics.

whole bunch of stuff buried underground; not just bodies, but monuments, irrigation systems (if you're "lucky" enough to have them), electrical, and more. Like everything we've talked about, those things don't just organize themselves. It's up to you to build a strategy that takes into account all of those factors, making sure the land is being used as efficiently as possible and that no issues arise due to lack of planning.

> *As a cemeterian, you have a big responsibility: caring for an eternal resting place.*

If you're not creating a comprehensive master plan or paying close enough attention, you could easily end up in a situation where you've plotted out an acre of land, grave by grave, without taking into account the fact that there's a tree smack in the middle of your site, irrigation will be blocked by upright monuments or benches, sidewalks aren't installed carefully to limit the loss of useful spaces, or irrigation main lines run too close to the section ... the list goes on.

There are other concerns here too. Some are maintenance related. For instance, are you putting trees too close to graves, where the roots will run out of room and end up toppling over, crushing everything in their wake? Some are about spacing. Are you taking into account any features you might have on site and eliminating plots where necessary (you can't really bury someone under a fountain)? Still others are about inventory or pricing. Are you accounting for the fact that a spot near that beautiful fountain should cost more than one in an open field, or are you losing that prime inventory dollar by charging the same rate for both? It may take some time and adjustments to get the strategy right, particularly with new sections in a cemetery—like pricing proactively so that the heart-level crypts and niches don't sell out first or increasing the retail price point of the graves closest to a water feature, for example—but it will almost certainly be worth your while.

Let's say you've master planned an acre of land. Inevitably, you sell a space right in the middle of it. This is the time for good procedures, for making sure you put that space right where it needs to be. Otherwise, you may end up in a situation where you've sold the last space in the row and find that you don't actually have enough room for the burial. I don't know about you, but I wouldn't want to be the one to get on the phone and explain to those family members that Dad won't fit in the plot that he's been promised next to Mom. It would be like selling a home in a development only to realize there's no room to build it, but worse, because that body has to go somewhere—and sooner rather than later. This is why lot/plot markers are essential.

Interment verification and records management fall under this umbrella too. You don't want to have a situation where those lot markers get switched and you've accidentally buried Sal in Jim's spot. While you're getting your plan in place—thinking about where things go and how everything works together—you have to consider the most important factor there is in any business: your customers.

Challenge the Way You Think about Customer Service

Take a moment and picture an old cemetery. You likely imagine rolling hills dotted with opulent markers, monuments, and mausoleums—big symbols of personal and familial legacies. Now, imagine a newer one. Do you still see those unique stones and buildings in your mind's eye? Probably not. Many newer cemeteries appear pristine and uniform, with flat identical markers designating graves. Cemeterians decided a while back that flat markers would make their lives easier. After all, it's much simpler to master plan—and mow and water the lawn—when you don't have anything to navigate around.

Uniformity has its benefits. However, when many of those cemeterians made a decision to improve their maintenance prospects, they also removed all of the personalization and uniqueness from family memorials. Instead, they embraced rules and regulations—enforcing a laundry list of things customers can and can't do. And along the way, they began to believe their businesses were exempt from the old adage that the customer is always right. Instead, they began telling their patrons whether or not upright markers were allowed; when they could visit; the times they could bring flowers; what types of flowers those could be; where they could place things on a grave, crypt, or niche; when those things would be picked up; what sections they could be buried in; and more.

Some of this is certainly justified, since the choices people make do affect the beauty for everyone. And much like a highly involved homeowner's association with a bevy of rules about what color paint people can use on their doorframes, with flat, uniform markers there's no need for families to worry about what would happen if someone bought the plot next door and decided to erect a hideous McMansion (or McMausoleum, as the case may be).

But with rising cremation rates and veterans' cemeteries offering plots that are essentially free, the competition is stiff. When we make things too difficult, buyers often decide to just go somewhere else. Customer-service guru John DiJulius often challenges professionals in every field to consider what they do and don't allow customers to do, particularly in an age where customers have more options than ever, and this is certainly relevant to cemeteries.

It's time to look at your list of rules and regulations and determine whether or not any of them are affecting the value of memorialization for your customer. You have to think about whether the decision to outlaw an upright memorial or prohibit their favorite flowers will affect a customer's decision. If it becomes too difficult to use the space and maintain their own desires, cremation—and taking those ashes with them—may suddenly seem much more appealing than choosing to do a burial with you.

The alternative, of course, is to do the opposite, offering families great and varied ways to memorialize someone special to them. It may indeed be time to concede, take down any signs stating your unnecessary rules, and customize the customer experience wherever you can. One way to do that is through product options.

Product Options

Unlike a funeral home, where you're buying all of your inventory as you need it and getting it delivered fresh, in a cemetery, you create it. You're building everything out and determining the options your customers have. Are you just selling ground spaces, or are you offering a wide array of products—private gardens, semiprivate gardens, scattering options, ossuaries, columbariums, indoor glass-fronted columbariums, private mausoleums, and more? Are you designating sections for different religious denominations for those who find that important?

There are a ton of ways to develop and market your property, and the more you make available to families, the more likely it is they'll be able to honor their loved ones in a manner that feels best to them. For example, when a cemeterian I knew opened up a new section that allowed upright memorials in a cemetery that had previously banned them, sales took off! He was able to charge a higher retail price for the graves, and incremental sales on memorialization increased as well. Considering all of the competitive challenges out there today, wouldn't it be worth it to drive additional revenue into your cemetery, even if it involves incurring some additional maintenance expenses?

Choice is important. If they don't have the option, they can't buy it. This is not the time to be bashful; you can have price points anywhere from $250 to $500,000. It may be the case that 99.9 percent of families who come to you find the idea that someone would spend $500,000 on a private estate outrageous. But if the right person comes along—that .1 percent—and they're ready to sign on the dotted line and slide over a huge pile of cash, you have to be prepared to accept it. You don't have to build a site fit for a queen (or oil tycoon) up front, of course, but if you make room for it in your master plan, the option remains available. Take the time to plot out where private estates or mausoleums could be developed, price them right, and train your sales team to be able to make the pitch. That way, you're ready to meet the needs of anyone who might walk through your doors, big spenders included.

When it comes to product options, it's not necessarily about selling so much as it's about providing the opportunity. Maybe your irrigation pond has plots around it that could be offered for sale along with custom mausoleums. Maybe the grassy hill on your property is the perfect place for scattering, if you designate it as such. The bottom line is that everything you offer has value. Once you give the customer the information, it's up to them to make the decision. Of course, when it comes to land care, that level of personalization does make things a bit more challenging.

Land Care

Back when I was working in Las Vegas, upright markers posed a real challenge for land-care management—especially if they were located right in front of a sprinkler head. Any grass behind those markers wouldn't get any water. With the desert heat beating down, that grass would take just a day or two to die and weeks to come back if we weren't careful. Upright markers weren't the end of the world, but they did require a bit of strategy. That's why we had an irrigation team, one tasked with keeping the cemetery green and beautiful.

Depending on where a cemetery is located, land-care concerns can be radically different, from cost to staffing needs. For example, I found great irony in the fact that in Las Vegas, where cremation rates are quite high, there is less of a need for cemeteries but the cost of maintaining one is much higher. Of course, cemeteries located in the Midwest and areas where there isn't a dearth of moisture don't have the same set of concerns. There, snow might pose more of an issue. No matter your circumstances, you have to think about land care and the ways you'll maintain the cemetery not just today or even ten years down the line, but in perpetuity.

It's also important to recognize that grounds people are often some of the hardest working people in our field, and they may be major contributors to the smooth operation of the business … if you let them. When I worked at a cemetery, it was such a humbling experience to work with the grounds team and to see just how much they did for the organization. With firsthand knowledge that the team was both hardworking and intelligent, I would share with them the financials—not the full statements but the expense side of things. Doing so enabled them to participate in the process and help find solutions to any issue we had with maintenance or beautification. When I showed them the numbers, they could easily see how much something like fertilizer cost. We could discuss why a particular expense was so high and what we could do to reduce it. And in the process, we not only lowered expenses but also increased buy-in. We fostered the kind of community and relationships that keep people happy and productive in their positions, all while keeping the land itself in tip-top shape.

It's amazing what an individual can do with information. The way that grounds people are treated by staff and families alike can be a real shame. When you can flip the script on any preconceived notions about your team and their ability to add value, you can do better, both by your staff and by the business at large.

Third-party land care has also become a trend over the past ten years. The trick is to determine whether outsourcing will allow you to improve the quality of the grounds, as well as save money. The other issue is to keep any concerns that arise on behalf of your staff in check. You may find that there are hard feelings, as often long-term employees have to be moved to another role or laid off when cemeterians decide to make the switch. If you do decide to go that route, it's important to ensure that the superintendent or foreman is engaged with the third party and holds that company accountable for performance, while managing any internal reactions.

It's not only grounds people who can help keep things beautiful. Customer-service tickets are also very important to address any land-care issues at a cemetery. When a customer comes into your office because a family member's monument is uneven or they'd like it cleaned, how are you following up on that request? If you have a system, you can see how the issue was resolved, when it happened, and who did what. Such a system might help you determine not only how well your staff is completing tasks, but also get to the bottom of what's really going on. Perhaps your employees are doing a great job, following up on tickets in a flash, but when the family comes back the next week, the flowers they ordered aren't there again. If everything is clearly described in your system, you may be able to follow that ticket and determine that the wind is actually the culprit.

Records management is also vital. A certain employee may be an expert at his or her job, keeping everything shipshape and holding on to all kinds of insights about the property, but what would happen if they were to be hit by a bus or call in rich after winning the lottery? You may know exactly how to handle the burial process, but if they haven't left their knowledge behind via records management, you won't have any recourse as to how things are currently being run. In many cases, people are doing this work for just $10 to $18 per hour, and if a life change comes up or they move for some reason, you have to make sure that knowledge doesn't go with them. In addition, if you have lots of paper files, it's important to invest in fireproof or online record storage. Past events have occurred in our profession where fires have ignited in funeral business offices and destroyed invaluable records, sometimes dating back one hundred years or more, crippling the owner's ability to run the business in the process.

Remember, too, that we will all move on at some point—whether it's to a different position or the great beyond. Meanwhile, that cemetery will still be there, ideally as lovely as the day the land was purchased. That's why good processes and procedures, both long term and short, must be part of the plan. That brings us to capital improvements.

Capital Improvements

Sometimes we forget that cemeteries are supposed to be forever and that, unfortunately, there's no material that will last quite that long. We end up building certain features because they look cool—a field of saplings, a set of burbling fountains, or a glassy lake, for instance, all of which may exude the peace and tranquility we're trying to capture. But you have to think about the life cycle of anything you build. And that means you also need a plan for preservation. Many of these features are outside and exposed to the elements, where a strong wind might blow all the trees down, a cold snap might freeze the pipes, or a glut of autumn leaves may clog a pump in your lake, giving you more of a swamp situation.

But it's not just the features that need maintaining. Having a proactive strategy to resurface and replace cemetery roads is especially important, as these are some of the most expensive capital improvements you'll have to make. If you don't have a plan in place to address any issues with your roads on the regular, you'll find yourself with an overwhelming—and exorbitantly priced—task to tackle.

To ensure you can keep a cemetery pristine for many lifetimes, you need to have a healthy perpetual care fund. Good cemeterians know that someday, that cemetery is going to be full, and they're still going to have to take care of it. So, they infuse that perpetual care fund beyond the state-mandated limit, either through donations from the community or by setting aside more of each sale. It's one way to show families just how much you care about maintaining the place their loved ones are buried. And that can be priceless. I think it's interesting that home buyers will have an interest in the health and care of the fund that a homeowner's association has for future maintenance of the neighborhood, but never once have I heard of a family asking about the status and health of the endowment care fund at a cemetery.

Park Potential

There is another benefit to operating a cemetery, and this one is already built in. Cemeteries are essentially parks—big, quiet, peaceful, grass-filled areas—and that means there are plenty of opportunities to host activities and promote them through social media. Memorial Park Funeral Home and Cemetery in Memphis, Tennessee, is a great example. It features the world's only man-made crystal cave and ten religious works of art, making it a frequent location for photographers and even weddings. Forest Lawn in Glendale, California, is another remarkable location. It has its own art museum, statuary, and two of the largest religious paintings in the Western Hemisphere on view, in addition to offering numerous services and events. As such, people who don't even have family members buried there visit all the time.

These are just a few examples, but they go to show that there's so much you can do with what you've already got. Think about how you might use your cemetery in different ways and connect to the community through events that may appeal to a much broader population than those who currently visit. Think back to my comments on establishing your different buyer personas.

As you can see, cemeteries are unique prospects. When you get to know all of the options in front of you, you can ensure you're using them to their fullest and find even more ways to innovate and keep business alive.

CHAPTER 8

Passing On: Effectively Navigating Succession

Think back to your hometown. Whether you moved away long ago or you're still in the house you grew up in, few if any of the same businesses you used to frequent as a kid are probably still around. The old-fashioned candy store you'd ride your bike to, the place where your parents used to buy your back-to-school shoes, even the local grocery store have probably given way to new purveyors. The stores that have taken their places may even be chains as opposed to mom-and-pop shops, depending on the area and just how much things have changed.

You've probably heard the adage, "From shirtsleeves to shirtsleeves in three generations." There's a lot of truth to it: with each generation, the likelihood of success drops. That's part of the reason so few of your favorite haunts are still around. Perhaps the people running that candy store or shoe shop had a greater knack for—or interest in—business than their children or grandchildren. As time passed, the subsequent owners just couldn't keep the business alive, if they wanted to at all.

If there's one holdout from your childhood, though, it's likely to be the community funeral or cemetery business (perhaps you're even the one running it!). We tend to have more longevity than other small businesses. There's just not the same kind of competition, and in small towns, tradition provides an additional layer of protection. The fact that customers don't visit very frequently also works to our advantage. While many people get tired of their favorite local restaurant and choose to check out other options, that's not happening with the local funeral home or cemetery. When their loved ones die, they call the same businesses they've always used—especially the cemetery, since any family members who have passed previously are there to stay.

But that shirtsleeves adage is certainly something to consider if you're thinking about leaving your business to the next generation—whether it's your children or your employees. If I haven't already beaten this point to death, I'll remind you again: preferences are changing. You have to make sure your replacements are prepared to keep up so your business can live on, even after you're gone. That's why building a succession plan is essential.

Maybe you haven't given much thought to what will happen when you're no longer at the helm. But whether your term comes to a halt because you decide to relocate to Boca Raton or simply end up underground, and whether it happens tomorrow or thirty years from now, you have to think about what's next. The time to do that is now. It's easy to put it off, especially if retirement—or death—seems like a distant arrangement. Instead, we imagine that no matter what happens, things will continue to work out. We believe that when we reach one inflection point or another, we'll simply recalibrate, dealing with it when the time comes. But you of all people know death doesn't work on a schedule. You have to be prepared on the off chance that the proverbial bus—or beer truck, if you prefer—is gunning for you one random Tuesday. Perhaps you'd rather imagine that you'll be magically transported to an island paradise. Either way, there has to be a succession plan in place so your staff or family knows what to do the day you don't show up.

If you're a service provider, especially in a funeral or cemetery business, it's easy to make it all about you. You're the one who connects with those families, closes the sale, and follows up with them after the funeral occurs. That feels pretty good on the ego when you're in the thick of it, but it's less great when you're ready to plot your escape. And if you haven't put the right processes and procedures in place, you won't be able to make a very graceful exit.

When you begin to think about succession, you have to determine what you're actually passing on, and it has to be more than just your name. Until then, the answer to the question of what will happen when you're gone is very simple: things will just fall apart.

If you insist on signing every check that goes out the door, refuse to share your trade secrets, or neglect to train your team to take on some of your responsibility, your business may die not long after you do, and it will probably be slower and more painful than you'd like. Thankfully, with a little planning, you can avoid this fate. You can protect your business so that it continues to prosper, giving the next generation the chance to be just as successful as you were, if not more so. It all boils down to making your service a product.

You can protect your business so that it continues to prosper, giving the next generation the chance to be just as successful as you were, if not more so.

Make Your Service a Product

In the funeral business, we rarely think of ourselves as providing anything other than a service. After all, almost everything we do is about action. We're solving the problem of death by picking up bodies, moving them somewhere, and doing something with them, whether that's cremation, burial, or shipment, and hopefully with a service! That's our value proposition. But any service can become a product if you institute clear and replicable policies and procedures. Just look at ride-sharing apps—with just a few taps on your phone, you can immediately book a ride home from the airport, specifying the type of car and timeframe in which you'd like it to arrive. Amazon offers the option to purchase home cleaning just like you'd buy paper towels. These companies have solidified and streamlined every aspect of these services, delivering their offerings in a consistent, easy-to-navigate format. And there are major benefits—not just for the customer, but also for the businesses themselves.

When you take a similar approach, you turn the tasks you may have been saddled with into a process that doesn't require your oversight. You become a franchise instead of a person, and suddenly you have a lot more bandwidth. You can do the things you never seem to have time to do, like turn your attention to business growth and innovation, and put yourself in a better position to move on.

Why? When you're getting a product, it doesn't matter who it's coming from. It's no longer about heading to Johnson Funeral Home or the local cemetery, where Jake's the guy everyone has to go see. That freedom can actually be a beautiful thing. In addition to giving yourself the gift of free time, you suddenly have a product that people can't get anywhere else. That product packs a lot more punch in terms of enterprise value.

Many funeral and cemetery business owners find this concept challenging, especially since community status plays such a large role in the work we do. However, if you want your business to succeed after your last day in the office, whether that day comes by choice or by necessity, making your service a product is an essential step. And though it may hurt your ego a bit to know that you're not irreplaceable, the fact that your business can continue on without you should provide some significant relief—in addition to the pride of knowing your legacy will live on.

To get started, identify your current policies and procedures—everything from the way information is shared to how you hire and fire and your accounting system. If any of them would cease to function if you didn't show up for work tomorrow, you need a new strategy.

Once you've sorted out the areas that need to be addressed ASAP, it's time to think about what's next. That includes determining whether your ideas for the future—particularly about who will be running things—are actually realistic.

Check In with Your Children

Many of us assume our children will join us when the time comes and eventually further our legacy, especially if we did the same for our parents. By the same token, those of us who don't have kids may believe a key employee will gladly take the reins. But—just in case you forgot—times are changing. If you're convinced your children or beloved staff members will be ready and willing to maintain that tradition but you haven't actually asked them about their plans, this is a good time to check in. Inquire as to what they want professionally and personally, and make sure you're listening when they answer. It may be difficult to hear their answers, especially if they'd prefer to head in a different direction, but when you know, you can prepare for the future—even if it's not the one you envisioned.

When you know where you're headed, you can start with the end in mind—a clear vision for what you want your business to be, even after you're gone. Otherwise, there's no way to realize it. Succession is a self-fulfilling prophecy, and if you haven't done any prophesizing, you'll be lucky if you succeed. It's as simple as that.

Ensure It's a Fit

Even if your child or subordinate is eager to become the boss, you have to ask yourself whether they are fit for ownership. We've talked about the fact that an employee isn't necessarily the right person to manage the whole business. What would they bring to the table, and how beneficial would they be to the business? You may truly love your son or daughter, but if he or she isn't capable of running things with training and support, it's important to be realistic about that—even if you know that's what they want. Just remember: denial is not a river in Egypt!

If you can understand the strengths and weaknesses of your potential successors as well as your own, you can better determine how to proceed. Looking for additional insight on whether or not your child would thrive as an owner? Gretchen Rubin's book *The Four Tendencies* is a great resource. Based on the concept that people tend to respond to expectations—both internal and external—in one of four ways, the book outlines each tendency and its implications for our behavior in any number of situations. And, according to Rubin, "understanding this framework lets us make better decisions, meet deadlines, suffer less stress and burnout, and engage more effectively."[12]

Those who are Upholders respond to both internal and external expectations similarly. They are as likely to meet a work deadline as they are to go after their own aspirations, like a New Year's resolution. This tendency can backfire, though, as Upholders tend to avoid quitting even when something isn't working. Questioners, the next group, want to understand the rationale behind any and every expectation, internal and external alike. If—and only if—they can grasp the logic of a particular move and they agree with it will they go along with it. Otherwise, it's a no-go. They'll

---

12   Gretchen Rubin, "About the Book." GretchenRubin.com. Accessed April 2, 2019. https://gretchenrubin.com/books/the-four-tendencies/about-the-book/.

typically meet their internal expectations, since they of course get the logic behind them, but if they don't agree with yours, they're not going to follow your lead. Meanwhile, Obligers are eager to live up to external expectations, but they have a hard time meeting their own. If they can create external accountability through supervision, deadlines, and negative reinforcement like late fees, they can thrive, whereas without them, they may have trouble getting out of bed. Rebels resist all expectations, no matter where they're coming from. Choice and freedom are most motivating to them.

The Four Tendencies provides information that everyone can use. The DiSC profile test can also offer helpful insights.[13] Either way, if you understand what characteristics your children or key employees demonstrate, you can make sure you're not setting them up to fail or putting them in a position they won't enjoy. If you've got a rebel on your hands, for instance, they may be better off doing something else. As parents (or caring employers, as the case may be), we of course have our own series of hopes and dreams for our potential successors. But in the end, the real question is whether or not they're happy. If they're conforming to a position that doesn't align with their natural tendencies, they're probably not going to enjoy it.

Figuring out that a child or key employee isn't really suited to run the business is not the end of the world—not at all. I've seen plenty of cases where the owners decide that their children or star staff member may not be the right fit to manage everything, but they are perfect for a particular role. So, they bring someone else in to run things. As a result, the next generation gets to do what makes them truly happy, like being out in the community, while someone else handles the day-to-day responsibilities. Thus, it's still possible to transfer things while compensating for any weak-

---

13 "DiSC Overview." DiSC Profile.

nesses they might have. And when you're proactive about it, everyone—owner, children, and staff—usually ends up happier in the end.

If your child does seem like the right fit, you also need to understand the realities of working closely with family. It's not the same as having employees who aren't next of kin. With family, the filters are far more limited, and when things go south, the gloves can come off. In the end, bringing your son or daughter to work may be okay for the business, but it might not be the best thing for your relationship.

Give the Gift of Outside Perspective

Convinced your child is the best person for the job? I always recommend that children who are slated to join the family business work somewhere else first, the way I did. When they're working in a place that isn't owned by Mom or Dad, they have to prove themselves in a real way—something that may not happen in their parents' operation. Why? Whether other employees mean to or not, they treat you differently when you're the boss's kid. If you're not careful, you can end up in a situation where people are letting your child operate unchecked—doing things they probably shouldn't be.

In addition to working elsewhere, your child should also be involved in any relevant associations, forums, or study groups, where they can get a chance to thoroughly understand the business with insight about the good and bad from others in the profession and connect with their peers. The people they meet will also be able to help guide them through the hurdles they'll encounter if the business becomes theirs.

As you plot out your succession plan, consider hiring a coach or consultant who can work with both of you. It's easy to be insulated within our profession—especially in the funeral business, where you may only have one other employee (if that). While you can provide great insight on the inner workings of your business, an outside source can be invaluable, helping your child evaluate whether certain practices are really the right way to go and determine how they can bring their own ideas and insights to the table to benefit the organization.

Getting more outside perspective in the form of a business valuation is helpful during this step too. It will give you a pulse on the financial health of your operation, letting you and your successor know what the present and future of your business could look like.

The next step in building a full picture for everyone involved is what I call a performance analysis. The performance analysis takes everything into account, not just the financials but also the four-legged stool—customer service, marketplace, workplace, and financial management. You have to make sure you're driving a culture of excellence. Otherwise, that successor is going to have a hard time taking over and creating one out of thin air. For more information on some of the factors Johnson Consulting considers, check out chapter 9.

Got everything sorted out? It's time to decide how this transaction is going to go down. In any buying situation, the seller should feel like they've gotten a little less than they should have (although JCG MNA clients get more), and buyers should feel like they've paid just a bit too much. That's the sweet spot. Otherwise, you're looking at a one-sided transaction, something that can be complicated to reconcile—especially in families. As such, both parent and child—or boss and employee—need to understand what they're giving up.

A Family Affair: Negotiating a Sale with Next of Kin or a Key Employee

Among the different types of buyers and sellers who come to Johnson Consulting are parents and children as well as owners and key employees. This arrangement comes with its own set of considerations. One primary factor both parties have to think about is that there is going to be a difference between the price an owner could get if they were to list their business on the market and what their child, sibling, or staff member will be able to pay for it. Why? That next generation is going to have more expenses than an outside buyer with centralized resources looking to add another business to their portfolio, whether it's an individual or a consolidation firm.

If you as the owner are not willing to recognize that added expense when you consider the value of the business and how much you're willing to sell for, you're going to make it very hard for your potential successor to make that purchase. To avoid some of the tension you might feel after the sale goes through, ask yourself whether you've set things up so that you have enough income to live on when all is said and done.

On the other hand, buyers have to make sure they're not obligating themselves to too much of a debt payment—one that probably wasn't there before the business was transferred to them, since it was probably paid off long ago. Whereas they're going to end up paying Mom, Dad, their boss, or the bank for years on end, in the past, things probably weren't run that way. If the business needed a new roof, new computers, or a new car, the owner just got them. With debt factored into the equation, your successors are really going to have to plan for any big expenses. They have to budget, keep an eye on the financials, and make sure the debt payments they're setting up are actually going to work.

Loan Structure

Once that's all set, it's time to think about structure. You may stipulate that your child gets a loan to cover the purchase price, or you may choose to structure the loan as an owner will carry (OWC). An owner carry may be particularly appealing if you don't have any debt on the business, which will allow you to have a first lien position as the seller. With this process, the owner provides the financing, rather than the bank. The buyer and seller agree on the terms of the loan, such as the size of the down payment (if there will be one at all), the interest rate (usually at or a little higher than the bank), and how long the buyer has to pay off the loan. There are a number of benefits here. Closing is faster and cheaper, since as the seller, you're determining the terms. The down payment amount is also flexible, because the agreement you have is the only thing governing it. This makes owner carry a good option for those buyers who would have trouble qualifying for a loan on their own too.[14] The other thing I like about it is that it gives the owner the first position on the lien on the real estate and the business. This way, if something happens, they can take everything back instead of a bank owning the business. Probably the nicest perk is that the seller usually gets the selling price they are looking for, if not a little higher, for accommodating the buyer by being the bank.

Whether they're paying the bank or their parents, buyers can make small payments over the course of many years, or they can make larger payments over a shorter period of time. I can definitely show a buyer how to overpay for a business and have plenty of cash flow: all they have to do is set something up where they're paying a debt for fifty years. By then, they'll have overpaid by way too much, but it will have been easy to make the payments. On the flip side, a buyer could agree on a payment term of just five years. They'll be done in no time, but in the interim, they'll hardly be able to live themselves, let alone make improvements to the business. The most recent loan terms I have been intrigued with are to offer a loan where there is no amortization. You accomplish this by offering a higher interest rate, let's say 3 percent higher than the going bank rates, then do an excess distributable cash sweep (EDC—the remaining cash the buyer could take after all expenses). The excess cash sweep can be in the range of 50 to 75

---

14   Jean Folger, "Owner Financing: Advantages and Disadvantages." Investopedia. February 2019. https://www.investopedia.com/articles/personal-finance/082815/pros-and-cons-owner-financing.asp.

percent of the excess cash. Those payments all go toward principal. Then do a five-year balloon whereby the buyer has to refinance or negotiate a new loan with the seller. This allows better success for the buyer early on and provides a great return for the seller.

When evaluating the terms of a loan and whether or not they'll work, think back to our discussion of debt service coverage ratios. The idea here is that the buyer doesn't want to have just enough to cover principal and interest—what would amount to 100 percent. If that were the case, all of the money coming in would have to go directly toward the debt. As such, they need more coming in.

That fixed charge coverage is a valuable formula here, because it's been proven by banks and financial institutions. It stipulates that as long as there is 140 percent—or even 125 percent in some cases—coming in, the buyer is probably safe. In smaller businesses, though, you have to be careful. That 1.25 is just a ratio. When you look at it as it relates to cash in a small business, you may be talking about an excess of only $3,000 per month. If your average sale is $6,000 per call and the business is off by just one funeral, there won't be enough money to pay the debt. If the business you own is similarly small, you probably want to aim for at least two times—or 200 percent of—your cash flow.

There are a multitude of scenarios; it all depends on your comfort and the paying ability and responsibility of the next generation. You also need to think about whether you need the money now or if you'd be happy to have those payments over a set period of time. And be sure, again, to consider what income you need to live on annually and whether having that money in the bank earning a return or offering that money as a loan to a buyer will be the best way to get your return. No matter what you determine, though, at some point, you have to let go.

Get Out of the Way—or Die Trying

If your succession plan is in place and your children, siblings, or key employee is slated to take over, it's time to get out of the way. Regardless of the circumstances of the sale, the bottom line is if you're not going to allow them to succeed on their own like you did, they're going to end up doing something else—especially if they have the entrepreneurial spirit that makes them interested in owning the business in the first place.

All too often, I see mothers and fathers who have sold to their children because they don't want to be involved anymore—in theory, at least. But then they end up staying in the loop, constantly micromanaging. They don't tolerate the shift well, prohibiting mistakes and new ideas alike; as a result, their son or daughter doesn't have the room to learn on their own. Without the formalities that interacting with someone who isn't blood can bring, they don't hold back either.

I've seen markets where there are two funeral businesses, each with the same last name on the sign. It's the same family, but at some point, someone went off and started another business because they just couldn't get along with their relatives. That's a worst-case scenario, because it means you're splitting the market while doubling the expenses. Additionally, if one party decides to sell, it can make negotiating the covenant not to compete hell on earth, since there are two different businesses operating under the same name.

How do you successfully transfer a business from generation to generation? Start now. It doesn't even matter if that son or daughter hasn't been born yet. When you start with the end in mind and work backward, you'll be able to see the amount of time you have to get it done. Often that realization is pretty sobering. A decade or two may seem like eternity, but—as you well know—life is short, and time certainly flies.

Whether you're passing your business on to the next generation or planning to sell it to the highest bidder, you need to get your house in order. That's how to prepare your business for the afterlife—life after you, that is. Next, we'll explore everything you need to know (and do) when there's a new owner in your business's future.

CHAPTER 9

Nearing Expiration: Determining When You're Ready to Sell

What's the best time to sell? People tend to believe that when the time is right, they'll feel it. They imagine they'll reach a point when their work doesn't offer them the same level of gratification, when they're burned out or ready to retire, or when a great offer falls right out of thin air. Maybe you've thought about the end of your run similarly. But the truth is if you haven't done any preparation, by the time any of those things happen, it's going to be too late.

Ironically enough, you may be ready to sell when you don't feel ready. Everything is in order. You have a pulse on your business and your staff—and you yourself still have a pulse (remember, that bus or beer truck could be just around the corner). That's when you get the most value for your business.

Of course, just because your professional house is in order doesn't mean your personal one is. Everything has to be aligned on that front, too, for the sale to work. No matter what you're feeling—or how far away a sell date seems—it's time to ask some questions:

- What would you like your life to look like after ownership, and how much money will you need to create that lifestyle? Think about the expenses that you take for granted: health care, medication, trips, cars, insurance, etc.

- At what age do you plan to retire? When you do, are you going to stay in the community or relocate to somewhere warm and sunny with plenty of mahjong and mojitos?
- And if you choose to hang around, do you plan on being involved in the business at any level to supplement your income?

Figuring all of this out may require you to get in touch with your financial advisor and sit down with your significant other and any family members involved in the business to talk about what's next. You wouldn't want to start the selling process with outsiders only to have your children decide they'd like to carry on your legacy, for instance.

There's a lot of soul-searching and family discussion that has to happen, but there's another factor that might dictate your plan: cold, hard cash. When it comes to navigating the nuts and bolts of the process, you have to understand just how much you will take home when you sell your business. And that means you need a specialist. Remember, too, that taxes are going to need to be paid for those gains on that sale. What money are you going to be left with? After all, it's not necessarily what you get, it's what you keep!

Seek Out a Specialist

Owners tend to come to their own conclusions about what their purchase price multiple might be. They have a rough idea of their cash flow and how they think the buyer might perceive it, and from there, they simply guess. I always find this interesting, as it is most likely their most valuable asset. Most all of us sell our residential homes using a specialist and don't even think about it. As funeral and cemetery professionals, we can be frustrated with the families that don't see the value we know we have. All this said, the same funeral professionals then may attempt to sell their business on their own. But there are a few issues here. First off, the value many owners imagine isn't accurate, because this isn't their wheelhouse. Most funeral and cemetery business owners don't run boutique investment firms specializing in mergers and acquisitions on the side. That's why it's so important to look for a specialist, especially when you're talking about the most valuable asset you own. Getting help and guidance on how to value your business and how to structure the transaction is the best money you can spend. That starts with a business valuation.

You also have to know not only the true value of your business, but also how those funds will likely be paid out. When you sell a business, there are three primary components: the money the buyer puts up outright, the loan they receive from the bank, and the amount owed under the covenant not to compete. All of that together adds up to the total sale price. Thus, it's possible that you're not going to get the full amount on the day of close. Some payments may be made over time. A portion of the sale price could be held back

> *Getting help and guidance on how to value your business and how to structure the transaction is the best money you can spend.*

for up to ninety days or more so that accounts receivables and payables can be reconciled and any remaining debt and other issues can be cleared out as you transfer your business to the buyer. Another piece could be deferred in a covenant not to compete that is fulfilled over the course of ten years. When you sell or succeed, you have to think about that.

Don't forget: even when you know the value of the business and understand how long it will take for the money to come through, there are also going to be tax implications. At the end of the day, when you know exactly how much you're going to receive, the results are almost always a little grim. It can be amazing how much the difference is. And it's that final amount that has to align with your goals for retirement and the legacy you want to leave behind. That's how you know if you're truly ready to sell or not.

If your business is doing well and you have debt you're working to pay down every year, look into that crystal ball. Stare deep into the distance—five or ten years out. Are you happy with where your business is likely to be? With the way you're spending your time?

Can't decide? It may be time to grab a Magic 8 Ball, too, and give it a shake. If sources say things won't look the way you want, it's time to consider selling now. On the other hand, if that ball is telling you "outlook good," you can continue to pay down that debt and maintain business as usual, since less debt means more money in your pocket when you hit the market.

Either way, it's time to start working on a task you may have thought you were going to avoid if you're looking for a bidder: building a good succession plan.

The Road to Success: The JCG Value Matrix

When you sell, even to an outside buyer, you're still on the hook for building a good succession plan so the people within your business and the buyer are able to seize the opportunities you've created and take advantage of the strong foundation you've laid. Otherwise, you'll be leaving behind a real mess. When you try to sell it, you're going to have a lot of explaining to do. Why? No one knows what to do other than you. And if you're selling to a consolidation company, they are going to want to know how you put things in place so they can maintain your success, often from afar. That means you have to do the work to make your service a product (flip back to the previous chapter for a refresher on how that's done) and have answers for any and all questions a buyer might have. Luckily, those efforts can also improve your business's value.

Value is at the crossroads of opportunity and risk. The more risks you put in front of a potential buyer and the less opportunity there is, the less value you're going to get for your business. Of course, the opposite is also true: more opportunity and less risk are very appealing,

Value is at the crossroads of opportunity and risk.

and as a result, those are the businesses that bring in the highest offers. Do you have a well-oiled machine on your hands, with good accounting practices and management, including general people and processes in place? If so, you're positioned to get a great value for your business.

At Johnson Consulting, we've put together the following JCG Value Matrix, which we use to determine the value of the businesses we work with. You can start your path to selling by getting a handle on each of these elements and making sure they're in the best possible shape prior to putting your business on the market. On the flip side, if you're thinking about buying, the matrix can help you determine whether the business you're looking at will fit the bill. Take a look at each of the categories, explained in detail in the pages to follow, and think about how your business stacks up.

JCG VALUE MATRIX
Location
Property Value
Property Condition
Functionality of the Funeral or Cemetery Business: Number of rooms, size, parking, entrance, chapel, hallway, etc.
Furniture, Fixtures, and Equipment (condition and quantity)

Autos (condition, quantity, leased/owned)
Demographics
Size of Market
Client Specificity (only serving a specific religion or ethnicity?)
Volume of Calls/Interments
Preneed Backlog
Case Count Trend
Market Share Trend
Mix Issues and Trends (cremation, alternative services, etc.)
Utility of Business: Full service vs. low cost only
Combo?
Top of Mind Aspect (brand)
Path of Progress: Integrating vs. disintegrating
Personnel: Asset or liability
Multiple Locations: Good or Bad Economies of Scale
Business Life Expectancy (general overall life expectancy, as well as for cemeteries the acreage that would sustain more than twenty-five years of business in a cemetery)

Location

To start, where are you located? Is your business on a busy street where you can hardly get into the parking lot because you have to cross a big four-lane road where speeding seems to be encouraged? Or are you in a sleepy area that's easy to access, if somewhat off the beaten path? The best location for a funeral and cemetery business is often somewhere between, just off one of those main four-lane thoroughfares, where things are just a little quieter but not hard to find—which can be a real blessing for people in a more emotional state.

Property Value

Property value can really change the way buyers look at a business, especially in markets with high real estate value like California and New York, so it's important to know what you're dealing with. It includes every physical aspect of your organization: land, facilities, cars, and more.

A high property value will help buyers finance and acquire your business. However, if the property has more value than the business itself, a new issue arises, and you have to look at things a bit differently. In this case, it's all about the *critical property*: the pieces of the property that are actually part of the business and that help drive the cash flow generated. Buildings you own that aren't necessarily part of the business—such as apartments—are nice to have, but they don't contribute to your organization's value. However, in small markets they may play a role in the small-town funeral home if the potential buyer could use it to supplement his or her living expenses.

If the property is worth more than the business, you have to determine whether or not you're going to lease the real estate and calculate the business value separately. When you're selling a business on its own, multiples are typically less, unless it's a very, very attractive opportunity with a strategic buyer or buyers.

Property Condition

When it comes to property condition, we're talking about the kind of shape your facilities are in. How are your parking lots, roofs, air-conditioning systems, carpets? If you've got a cemetery, how are the roads, grounds, water features, fencing, irrigation systems, and more? Is everything in good condition? If not, are you planning to do anything about it?

Functionality

How functional is your funeral business, and does it reflect the interests of the community in which you're located? The size of your building, types of rooms you have, chapel, hallway, entrance, reception center, and even parking lot all affect the functionality of your facility.

If your cemetery business has virtually run out of room or doesn't have the bandwidth to expand into the more traditional high-end business that customers are looking for in your area, what does that mean for your buyer? If your funeral home doesn't have a reception area and instead you suggest that guests gather in your visitation room for a meal, how likely is it that they will recommend your service to their friends? If you answered, "not very," you understand just how important functionality is to your overall value.

Furniture, Fixtures, and Equipment

The condition of your furniture, fixtures, and equipment matters too. If you have rooms full of old, musty furniture, dated fixtures, and decades-old equipment in your funeral home, or broken backhoes, rusty lowering devices, and decrepit mowers at your cemetery, buyers won't necessarily be champing at the bit to pay top dollar, since they'll have to step in and do some remodeling and upgrading. A caution to this, though—depending on the repairs or improvements needed, sometimes you can still get full value for the business if it is attractive enough; it just depends.

Autos

Are your vehicles leased or owned? Like property, leased ones are less appealing than those you own. If they're all yours, how many do you have? Would you say it's more or fewer than you need? What kind of condition are they in? How are you taking care of them? Remember, even if your vehicles are paid for, there are still annual maintenance expenses associated with them—which will only grow over the years. Here's another thing to think about: for every $1,000 in vehicle lease expense, that is a reduction in purchase price of roughly $5,500–$6,000. Consider whether the vehicle leases are adding or hurting value when compared to their purpose and need.

Demographics

With a handle on the physical aspects of your business, let's talk about demographics. Are the demographics in your community holding steady or changing? If you're in the Northeast, maybe older community members are fleeing at record levels, finding that they prefer retirement communities and tropical heat waves to drafty farmhouses and six months of blizzards. Perhaps you're in an area that's attracting a lot of new blood because there's a booming tech business in town. Those employees won't stay young forever, and they'll probably have a different perspective on what they'd like their funeral or cemetery arrangements to look like than the people you've served in the past. How are you taking these changes into account?

Market Size

Your market size has a big impact on value too. A small market requires a certain type of buyer, one who can maintain relationships within the community. That can make them trickier for consolidators and outsiders, who don't always have the bandwidth or experience to cultivate the network necessary for success. On the other hand, in larger markets, many families may not have even known who the owner was in the first place, making it much easier for a new buyer to come in and compete well against the competition.

Client Specificity

Here, we're talking about the religion or ethnicity of the people you serve. Do you reach a diverse population, or does your business serve only one section, such as Jewish or African American families? How does client specificity tie into your own identity? In the funeral business, barriers are falling, and you have to have a plan to address any of the separation occurring in your own organization. Are you becoming familiar with other communities within the market you're serving and adjusting your offerings to address their needs?

Volume of Calls/Interments

The higher the call volume or number of interments, typically the bigger the revenues and the more impact a new buyer can have as they come in. This affects opportunity, making it an important stat for buyers.

Preneed Backlog

When it comes to your preneed backlog, there are three factors to consider:

- How much is in the file cabinet, or the amount of future business you have already secured through preneed sales.
- How much comes out of the file cabinet each year, or the number of preneeds that become at-need.
- How much you put back into the file cabinet annually in the form of new sales or contracts.

These three numbers dictate future success and market share of the business. Looking for benchmarks on how to secure value through preneeds? Active funeral businesses usually have three or more times the annual revenue. However, keep in mind that a high preneed-fulfillment ratio (anything over 33 percent) can be tricky, since it means you have to be able to prove that you can sustain it with new sales year after year.

In addition, do you have any guaranteed unfunded preneed agreements? These can obviously negatively impact the value of the business due to the liability to deliver on them when the death occurs. In a cemetery, the preneed merchandise and services must be set aside in trust. Based on your state legislation, have you withdrawn a portion of the trust funds prior to delivering some of the merchandise and services? If so, it will have an impact on the overall valuation. These are all things to keep in mind when putting your operation up for sale.

Case Count Trend

Case count refers to the amount of business you do on an annual basis. In a cemetery, you are looking at the number of full-body and cremation interments your business does on an annual basis. What does the trend look like over ten years? This gives buyers a bigger picture of how your business has been serving the community over time. Obviously the better the trend, the more the interest, and therefore the better the value.

Market Share Trend

How do you hold up against your competition? Are you bringing in the same number of cases? Fewer? More? Do you have anything they don't, or vice versa, and do you have a plan to address your place in the market going forward? I like to say that a healthy market share profile is one where a buyer can see that you compete well against diverse competition, including low-cost businesses in your area. If you have no competition and the market is ripe for one, that can scare a buyer and affect value (even though for you, life is good at the moment!).

Mix Issues and Trends

Speaking of which, everyone in our business is dealing with the rise in cremation. How does your mix trend look? Is it stable? Are cremation rates rising faster in your business than in others, or are changes coming more slowly? The best businesses are adjusting to meet customer preferences, with a plan to address any shifts moving forward.

Utility of the Business

Is your business full service, providing as many or nearly as many burials as cremations, or is it a low-cost operation, exclusively offering discounted cremation or burial options? The utility of a business affects value. While the former type is deeply tied to goodwill, the latter is strictly associated with price. It's a business model that lives and dies on velocity, which has to be significant to turn a profit—one with much leaner margins than its full-service counterparts. Thus, low-cost businesses can pose some risks. For one, if someone enters the market with an even lower cost, there is no name in place to protect you, and it may be something that dissuades a buyer from signing on the dotted line.

Combo

"Combos" refers to funeral homes located on cemeteries. If you have both facilities in one place, you're a one-stop shop, which has its own appeal. Of course, not all combo units are equal, but it's certainly true that larger funeral–cemetery combo locations are the ones that get the highest purchase prices we've seen since the inception of Johnson Consulting. Why? Case mixes are a little more insulated—burial rates remain higher because the cemetery itself attracts those interested in them. In addition, once heritage is established at the cemetery, people just keep coming back. Those factors increase opportunity and reduce risk for a potential buyer.

Top of Mind Aspect

Whether or not you're a one-stop shop, it's crucial to cultivate brand recognition. Are you the leading brand in your market? Do families come to you because you've been the trusted name in the business for years? Those businesses get good value. If not, it's time to think about your marketing plan and address anything that could be preventing you from occupying more space in the market.

Path of Progress: Are You Integrating or Disintegrating?

The path of progress refers to the current position of your business and where you will be in the future. As you look at your market, where is the population moving? Are you right in that path, or, as some would say, are you on the right side of the tracks for your customers? If not, do you have a plan to get there? Look out five to ten years, and if you don't like the answer, it is time to start thinking about what to do!

Personnel: Asset or Liability?

When it's time to sell, your employees can be an asset or a liability, depending on their values, skill, and age, among other characteristics. At Johnson Consulting, we are currently in the process of valuing some organizations staffed with employees who are in their seventies and eighties. In the funeral business, it's possible to still be relevant at that age, but the fact is, mortality is not on your side—or on that of the buyer.

Plus, we have seen, at times, that many older employees decide to retire when the business sells. They say to themselves, "If Joe's out, so am I," and often, there's a wealth of knowledge and relationships that go with them. If some of the key people in your organization are nearing their own expiration dates, the risk for potential buyers is higher. Meanwhile, if your staff is relatively young and open to change, your organization may be more appealing than the competition. This is a tough one because of our nature of being caregivers. We want to keep some of those older employees on because they have been so good to us. The good news is that they still can help with the organization; however, a succession plan for them needs to be in place before an issue occurs that can affect the value of your business.

Multiple Locations: Good or Bad Economies of Scale?

Do you have multiple businesses? If the answer is yes, how successful is each location? If you're keeping a business open simply because it was your original operation and closing it would take an emotional toll, you have to determine whether running it is a good use of your time.

If the real estate is worth more than the business itself and you're spending 80 percent of your waking hours working on it with little or no impact to your bottom line, having that extra location isn't doing you any favors.

Business Life Expectancy

Last, remember that nothing is truly forever—not even cemeteries. Businesses have life expectancies, too, and the probable length of yours will have an impact on your perceived value. Where is the business headed? Is there any competition in the market, new or old, and if so, are you competing well against them? Your answer will help to determine the risk for a potential buyer. Keep in mind that if you're leasing your building, it's more of a gamble since the land you're on almost certainly won't be yours—or your successor's—for the long haul. Meanwhile, cemeteries that are within a few years of being sold out are much riskier propositions than ones with twenty-five years or more of inventory.

If your business is on solid ground in all of these areas, with plans for the future, you may just be ready to sell—whether you want to or not. On the flip side, if you're thinking seriously about selling right now and there are elements of your house that just aren't in order, you have some work to do.

If you're not happy with the outcome of this exercise, don't be discouraged! There are plenty of ways to get the kind of result you want. Let's take a look at some case studies from Johnson Consulting's files to see how all of this has the potential to play out.

CHAPTER 10

Happily Ever Afterlife: Case Studies on Buying, Selling, and Creating Successful Strategies

Death always marks an ending—though it's rarely a happy one. Unless you're in the funeral and cemetery businesses, that is. At Johnson Consulting, we've seen plenty of positive outcomes in death care, particularly when it comes to buying and selling businesses, as well as instituting systems, people, and processes to increase efficiency and value.

Making a change in your business—whether you're thinking about buying, selling, or simply streamlining things—can spook anyone, but the following case studies show that with the right insights and support, the funeral and cemetery service professions are not exempt from a fairy tale conclusion.

Selling Success Stories

At Johnson Consulting, we see success stories every day, especially when it comes to sales. Consider the case of one client in the mid-Atlantic region who came to Johnson Consulting for a valuation. He didn't feel ready to sell, but he was at a crossroads and wanted to make sure that as he moved forward with the strategies of his business, he knew what his baseline was.

He was pleasantly surprised by how much we determined his business may be worth, but he still didn't feel ready. Instead, he asked about areas where he could improve so that he could boost the business value even further. We gave him our take, explaining that he could likely cut down on payroll expenses, among other areas.

He was also thinking about buying another business and asked whether it seemed like the right time. "Well," we told him, "not if you're going to pay more than the value multiple we come up with."

We gave him perspective on what we thought the multiples were using the JCG Value Matrix (turn back to the previous chapter for a reminder if you need one). He determined that he would be able to pay less than the value multiples we had assigned to his business, knowing that even if he sold within six months, he would actually make money on the transaction.

A short time later, things got a bit slow. For the first time in a while, he had the opportunity to spend more time at home as a husband and a father. The opportunity served as an aha moment about what his life could look like with a little more breathing room. So, eight months after we finished the first valuation, he reached out to us to update it.

With the number he got, he decided he was ready to test the market. Johnson Consulting also has a unique marketing process that allows us to build a story for buyers, which would create additional value and further bolster the positive changes he had implemented since the last time we talked. We sent the information out to potential buyers to see what their reactions would be. When we called to present him with an offer, he was quiet for a moment. The number was high, likely much higher than he had anticipated. "I gotta get back to you," he said, and all but hung up.

He had realized there was a decision to be made whether or not he was completely ready to make it. It had become apparent that this was indeed a very good time to sell—something he only knew because he had decided to get a valuation a handful of months earlier.

We suggested he do some thinking about what he wanted, including looking into that crystal ball and determining what his business might be like five or ten years down the road. We also suggested he think about what he wanted in terms of his quality of life. Ten years from then, he would be in his sixties. It was hard to imagine, but he thought he might want a slower existence, with more time to spend with his wife and any grandkids that might come along.

After weighing all that, he got back to us. "You know," he said, "I wasn't planning to sell. I don't need to sell. And quite honestly, I don't really want to. But from everything you're telling me, it sounds like I should."

Unlike many owners who find themselves in a position where they have to sell and end up stuck, he went into the situation proactively. And with enough information and concrete numbers on the table, he was able to make a thoughtful decision.

In the end, he sold for a very high purchase price and ended up taking a position with the new owner moving forward, in which he could pull in a nice salary without the stress or strain of running everything on his own. The buyer was also very satisfied with the purchase, and Johnson Consulting had the privilege of seeing a successful transaction. There were wins all around.

Of course, that's not always the case. Owners frequently explore the possibility of selling because of a particular issue. That was the situation for another client of ours who owned a business in the south-central part of the country. He didn't own the real estate his operation occupied, and he felt stuck. He was tired of dealing with the landlord. Every year, the prices went up and the building manager seemed less responsive to his needs. Still, the business was humming along. He was using our accounting, metrics, and surveying systems and had made changes early on based on the feedback we provided, reducing his payroll expenses by redistributing responsibilities among his staff. He had no reason to sell other than his frustration with the property. But some days, that felt like reason enough. Knowing that businesses occupying leased buildings typically have lower values, he was curious about the kind of multiples he would see. So, we helped him put his operation on the market.

When the offers came in, he was thrilled. Part of the reason he was able to get such a high price was because of the adjustments he had made based on the benchmarks we provided. The payroll efficiencies alone equated to $150,000 to $200,000 in cost savings. All told, $1 million to $1.5 million of the purchase price he received was solely due to the efficiencies he got from adapting his practices according to our insights in accounting and consulting services. I can assure you that our fees did not total $1.5 million. In fact, he probably paid less than $150,000 in all the years he worked with us.

After he sold, he was given a key role in the business making a nice salary, with benefits and other perks. In the end, the accounting benchmarks, survey results, and metrics he utilized all added up to exceptional value for him, regardless of his lack of owned real estate.

Another client in the Southwest experienced the impact of implementing high-quality management services. He used every service Johnson Consulting offers—accounting, strategic planning, consulting, surveys, and sales analysis. When he was in his late fifties, he decided to use our acquisition analysis service as well. He had been in a rut when he first decided to begin acquiring businesses. Acquisitions are fun, but they require a lot of data and accounting efforts. We helped him make the process as easy as possible for the firms he purchased.

Eventually, he became curious about the value he could get for his business, so we gave him our thoughts. Because everything was running so smoothly, the tasks necessary were less painful when he decided he was ready to move on. We collaborated with him on the adjustments and built a marketing package out of the data we had been collecting over the years to help explain the opportunity a buyer would have in purchasing his businesses. He got a very good value for his operations and won't have to work another day in his life. Today, he's a very happy former owner.

Buying Bliss

Buying also offers the potential to win big, as one client by the name of Scott Pontone learned. He came from a family of casket salesmen. Though he had been in the funeral business his whole life, Scott had primarily been an investor. But he was interested in exploring funeral home ownership. So, he came to Johnson Consulting and brought us in on the first deal he wanted to make.

My team and I met with him and provided our thoughts on the structure of the sale. We then found him a lender who was interested in offering assistance. Scott decided to go ahead and buy the business. Then, because he didn't have direct experience as a funeral home owner, he asked us to integrate the accounting and onboarding, provide consulting services and conduct surveys and sales analysis, work on the strategic plan, and report back. The first purchase went wonderfully, and once the business was up and running under his management, he asked us to work on the next one.

Today, his staff handles the day-to-day operations in his business, but we handle all of the reconciliation, audits, controls, accounting, customer surveys, and reporting. As a result, he's not saddled with the same responsibilities that most funeral business owners are and instead lives a life that many owners probably couldn't imagine. Whereas others believe they're the only ones who can run their operations, Scott knows that's simply not the case.

Another client also experienced major gains when he decided to buy. At the time, he owned two funeral home locations. There was a cemetery right between them, and he thought it might be a good idea to purchase it. So, he asked if Johnson Consulting would reach out to the current owner and see if she was interested in selling. The owner was amenable to the idea, and we did a workup of the potential value. Our client bought it and started achieving synergy between the two funeral homes on either side of the cemetery.

He began directing customers there while implementing all of our programs to reenergize the culture of the cemetery. Eventually, he sold the cemetery back to its former owner, along with both of his funeral homes, for a profit. It was an excellent demonstration of how cemeteries can be a good investment when you play your cards right.

If you have one or more funeral businesses in the same area, you can ensure synergies between them, driving families toward the cemetery, and even determine whether building a funeral home on site may be a good idea. In this client's case, buying the cemetery helped him to connect and build his businesses in a way that definitely paid off.

Yet another client found success in a similar manner. Early on in my career at Johnson Consulting, I found a cemetery listing for just $50,000 for a client of mine in the Midwest. It was a sleepy little place that had been virtually inactive for years. In fact, it was for sale in what was essentially the classifieds in our sector—not at all where you'd find a high-performing business for sale. But my client already owned a number of funeral homes nearby, and he figured this cemetery could be a great addition to his portfolio. He bought it, cleaned it up, and started directing those customers who wanted a traditional burial there.

When all was said and done, the cemetery—in conjunction with his existing businesses—sold for about ten times what he had originally paid for it.

These situations demonstrate that when you understand the value of your business, buy something at or under that value, and build in the right efficiencies, when the time comes to sell, you'll be able to do so for more money than you may have imagined possible.

Survey Results to Die For

Surveys can also have a significant impact on business success, as one of our large consolidation clients learned. The company bought a number of former consolidator-owned firms through Johnson Consulting. When they bought, there was some absentee management going on, and arrangers were basically operating on their own. The new manager needed a quick way to check in and get a feel for how each arranger was operating, particularly because it's a closed-door environment; he couldn't be there to see and hear what was happening. By surveying customers, though, he could get the inside scoop.

A thorough survey program like ours could show the manager who was doing a great job and who was not. The manager invested in the JCG Performance Tracker survey and sales analysis program and let it run for sixty days. It quickly became evident that certain arrangers were consistently receiving poor scores. Based on the information we provided, he decided to make some staffing decisions, letting go of one arranger and instituting some trainings for others. This move alone increased the business's customer satisfaction level within six months.

Another measure we track that helped in this case is the Net Promoter Score (NPS), which was designed by Bain Consulting. Basically, if your firm is running at 75 percent NPS, that means that 25 percent of your current call volume/interment rate is at risk to be stolen from the competition. Run the math on that with revenues and profits and it gets people's attention.

What does that mean in terms of value? Think about the price of a single customer won or lost—a potential $20,000 in enterprise value.

Who knows how many $20,000 customers the company has harnessed or maintained just by making one small adjustment to their staffing? In this case, we determined that if each arranger boosted their average sale to match that of the firm at large, they could drive 12.9 percent in additional revenue—nearly all profit—to the company!

On the flip side, how many had been lost previously? The manager would never know. Thus, living—and dying—by the results of our surveys helped the manager drop some, well, dead weight—and potentially improve the company's bottom line.

Fortunate Fixer-Uppers

There are also plenty of situations we've encountered where a little analysis and strategic planning go a long way. Take one client in the Northwest, for instance, who requested a general health check on his business's financials. He owned a premier firm, but things just weren't operating the way he thought they should be, and there were a number of reasons as to why. The firm was suffering in part because a discount operation had moved into town—a community that had a very high cremation rate to begin with. The owner had also bought a funeral business that turned out to be a challenge and was grappling with the fallout from that decision. In addition, the firm's payroll was completely out of whack at around 50 percent of net sales, but the owner couldn't imagine a single role that could be cut. Despite all of these challenges, he wanted to reach a point where he could eventually bring in enough money to retire.

We began with a strategic planning session, where we interviewed the staff and offered guidance on how the owner could reengineer the organizational chart, shifting around responsibilities and eliminating unnecessary roles. There had also been staff members on the team who had been influencing the culture for the worse, spending 80 percent of their time on 20 percent of the valuable workload. Some of them needed to go. The owner had thought that rightsizing the payroll wasn't possible, but with a few tweaks, we were able to do it.

We also integrated metrics into the business, including the JCG Performance Tracker survey and sales analytics, and provided accounting assistance so that the owner was able to alter the overhead structure of his accounting department. After those changes were made, the business was able to operate at a whole new level. But it took time for it to reach peak performance. The owner had to pay down some of his existing debt, restructure the organization, and develop a plan—with our help—to compete with the local discounter. He eventually decided to buy out one of his competitors and move into their building, all while developing a clean set of financials to show future buyers the path he had taken to get there.

Not long ago, the owner made his last debt payment and asked for a valuation. We are in the process of conducting it, but it looks like he is going to get everything he wanted—including a payout that will allow him to retire stress free. And with everything taken care of in terms of the organization, it's just a matter of deciding when to pull the trigger on the sale. Because he's reached a point where he doesn't have to sell, he has the opportunity to see what the market has to say and decide what to do based on the offers he receives.

The services he's accessed through Johnson Consulting have added $500,000 to $1,000,000 to the business's cash flow, and probably about $2 to $3 million to the purchase price. How much did he pay us over the course of our relationship for all that added value? No more than $250,000.

Another client came to Johnson Consulting to address their profitability. They knew it was low. And while they wanted to reinvest in the business and find growth, they simply didn't have very much cash available to do it. We conducted a financial management review, addressing budgeting, expenses, payroll, marketing spend, and more. At the end of their last fiscal year, their EBITDA had been $278,978—6.6 percent of their revenue. With a plan for budgeting, marketing, and payroll in place, by the end of the following year, their profitability increased to $676,555, or 15.1 percent of revenue. From an enterprise standpoint, with $398,000 in additional cash, this firm increased their enterprise value by more than $2 million. Happily ever afterlife indeed. Again, I can assure you that the cost of our services was pennies compared to the value increase.

The Power of Pricing

Integrating different strategies can also have a tremendous impact on the success—and value—of a business. For instance, many people think raising prices is just that: raising prices. But by doing it strategically by reviewing your pricing, thinking critically about the way those goods and services are packaged, and training your staff on your offerings, you can influence the average sale without ever raising prices. You certainly don't have to be a hardcore salesperson—no arranger or director I've met has been designed to do that. Instead, it really comes down to comfort in front of the family and making it as easy as possible for them to make a decision. As such, packaging your products and services can go a long way. Johnson Consulting often works with firms to institute strategic pricing initiatives, and the results demonstrate just how powerful a little strategy can be. Consider the following example:

We began working with one firm to address pricing in 2015. When we first looked at their data from January through June of that year, their average at-need burial was $7,460 and their average at-need cremation was $3,052. We helped them launch their new pricing initiative the following month, discussing opportunities for packaging and ways that staff could communicate their offerings to families. We helped them reconstruct the general price list—incorporating packages—while still complying with FTC standards, changed the merchandise available in the display room, and incorporated training for staff on how to present their offerings to customers. By November of the same year, the average at-need burial had reached $8,144 and at-need cremation was up to $3,374.

The spread in average sale for cremation was about $320. Let's say this is a two-hundred-call funeral home. That $320 per sale—which is likely all profit—translates to an infusion of $64,000 directly to the bottom line. With a six times value multiple applied, you're looking at a $350,000 to $400,000 increase in enterprise value! It just goes to show how much arrangers or directors—and the customer service and packaging they provide—can impact enterprise value and, ultimately, the sale price of the business.

It just goes to show how much arrangers or directors—and the customer service and packaging they provide—can impact enterprise value and, ultimately, the sale price of the business.

And the results of implementing strategic pricing initiatives can be even more significant. Consider another firm we worked with during the same year. Before Johnson Consulting came in, they were bringing in $8,150 on average for at-need burials and $2,697 for at-need cremations. They incorporated all of the strategies listed in the previous example, as well as an incentive compensation plan. Rather than basing bonuses on sales, they used the incentive program to prioritize getting high customer survey marks, showing the customer the full range of services and products, and collecting money. When they did, the average at-need burial sale was bumped up to $9,057 and at-need cremation soared to $3,510. That's basically a $900 increase. In a two-hundred-call firm, you're looking at an additional $180,000 to the bottom line, or about $950,000 to $1,050,000 in enterprise value. And in terms of what it cost them to engage in the pricing initiative, it was pennies on the dollar for what they got out of it.

You may feel that things are dead set where they are, but as you can see, that doesn't have to be the case. The real-life scenarios above show that there's plenty of potential to buy and sell successfully and address any issues that may be preventing you from reaching peak profitability. With some analysis—potentially from an outside source who can give you good perspective—and some effort, you can bring new life to your business.

With all that potential in mind, let's pick up our trusty crystal ball and take a look at what the future has in store for the funeral and cemetery service professions.

CHAPTER 11

Kingdom Come: Exploring What's Next in Funeral and Cemetery Services

Everyone has their own take on what happens after death, but what about the future of the profession itself? What does the great beyond of the funeral and cemetery businesses have in store? We know things are changing; that may very well have been the reason you picked up this book. And if you didn't know before you started reading, you certainly do now. Death will come for all of us one day, but the way families are dealing with that fact—and solving the problem of what to do with those who have passed—is shifting. From the trends we're seeing today, we can make some predictions about what the future of death care will look like and use that knowledge to our advantage. It all begins with acknowledging the rise in cremation rates.

Ashes to Ashes—A Cremation-Focused Future

While cremation rates crossed over the 50 percent mark in 2016, many professionals—including the National Funeral Directors Association—believe they'll hit 80 percent by 2035.[15] That may sound exorbitantly high, but you may remember that my funeral home in Sun City, Arizona, is already there. Of course, in some small markets, burial rates may hold out a little longer, but eventually most of us will go up in smoke. In Japan, for example, 99.99 percent of people are cremated.[16]

There are numerous reasons for the rise, many of which we've covered in this book. For one, the US is becoming less religious overall, with fewer people maintaining the traditions they were brought up with. Catholics would never have considered cremation back in the day. But it's since been approved by the Church itself and become the norm. And while Judaism has barred cremation and many would have considered the practice transgressive just a handful of years ago, more than half of Jews are choosing this method today.[17]

The fact that we tend to move far from home, sprawling out across the country and even the world, makes it difficult to engage in traditional memorialization at the local cemetery, where generations have been laid to rest, and contributes to the popularity of cremation as well. In many cases, there just isn't anyone around to attend a funeral service or visit a grave with any frequency. Even when people do decide to memorialize their loved ones, the circumstances have changed. Whereas it used to be that someone died on a Tuesday and the funeral was held by Thursday or Friday of the same week, more and more funeral homes and cemeteries are seeing services delayed for two weeks or more—not only to create a meaningful event but also to comply with everyone's travel schedule.

---

15 Annabelle Gurwitch, "Cremation Nation: Our New Way to Go." *The Wall Street Journal*. March 2019. https://www.wsj.com/articles/cremation-nation-our-new-way-to-go-11553880025.

16 Hiatt, Anna. "The History of Cremation in Japan." JSTOR Daily. September 2015. https://daily.jstor.org/history-japan-cremation/.

17 Gurwitch, "Cremation Nation: Our New Way to Go."

More and more services are being held outside of the funeral business too. It's not a place that families want to be, so they simply choose to go elsewhere. Rather than remembering Uncle James or Auntie Mabel in a subdued chapel on your property, people are honoring the lives of their loved ones at the churches they attended every Sunday, the country clubs they frequented, and even in their own homes. But if you can adapt, providing the kinds of products and services that support these changing preferences, you'll prosper in this business.

Considerations for Cemeteries

Often, families don't realize that when they choose cremation, there's still a body there—it's just in ash form. And that means they need to do something with it. While they may choose to put it on their mantel and simply pass it down from generation to generation, there are many other choices, and cemeteries could play a big part in offering those.

Cemeteries that are—and will continue to be—successful are doing a number of things to keep up with the times. As discussed in chapter 7, some are embracing their status as beautiful parks, especially since development in cities is ever increasing. It's not as much of a stretch as you might imagine for people to get over the fact that there are a bunch of dead people in the ground and enjoy cemeteries for the terrific green spaces they are. And when they do, they frequent these cemeteries for the exciting events they're hosting. From artwork to historical displays and even laser shows, movie nights, and Fourth of July fireworks, savvy cemeterians are using their grounds to the fullest and turning a profit.

They're also recognizing the rise of cremation and making sure the preference is reflected in their options. When I worked at Palm Mortuaries and Cemeteries in Las Vegas, Nevada, the business offered numerous options for those who chose cremation. There was the garden of meditation, complete with a cenotaph where families could store their urns and have their loved ones' names inscribed. There were also areas where ashes could be scattered, a columbarium, and semiprivate and private gardens. Providing an array of choices gives families a sense of comfort, knowing that Mom can be somewhere other than their hall closet and they can still visit her from time to time in a beautiful, well-cared-for space.

Choosing a place for cremains doesn't rule out other options either. Some of those ashes could still be placed in a keepsake or transformed into a diamond. And whether or not you're in the cemetery business, it may not be long before your customers are asking for similar treatment.

> *Providing an array of choices gives families a sense of comfort, knowing that Mom can be somewhere other than their hall closet and they can still visit her from time to time in a beautiful, well-cared-for space.*

The more normalized cremation becomes within our culture, the more people will become comfortable with the plethora of unique disposition options out there—whether they decide to send Grandma to the moon or have her ashes turned into ink for their latest tattoo. Are you equipped to fulfill their wishes?

Addressing the Impact of Discount Operations

Rising cremation rates won't just pose a challenge for those of us who have been in the business for generations. The discount direct cremation businesses (or "cremation discounters") arriving in the market need to tune in too. Why? At Johnson Consulting, we see firsthand how little profitability there can be in these businesses. Discount direct cremation is not a business model so much as it's a job—one with very high liability. We can't forget that it's an irreversible process. Other funeral businesses certainly have similar issues with liability, but it's built into their pricing. Businesses that aim to deliver a low-cost, no-frills experience don't have the same luxury. States will have to think about how they plan to regulate these businesses, determining the necessary qualifications owners and staff must have to protect those who choose to use their services.

On the other hand, if you're a traditional provider in a market with cremation discounters, you have to consider how you will keep up. A lot of businesses are putting their own low-cost options into place. Though they probably won't make much money on the discount operations themselves, providing those services allows them to compete in their markets and hold on to the families they have served in the past whose preferences may be changing.

Despite the threat cremation discounters pose today, as cremation rates rise, pricing across the profession will also have to change. If the cremation rate were to hit 100 percent tomorrow, I wouldn't hesitate to bet that prices would almost double in short order. In those places where cremation rates are higher than in the US, such as Europe and Asia, average sales are as high or higher than they are here. For example, in Japan—where cremation is about as close to 100 percent as you can get—the average cost of cremation and disposition is around $31,650.[18]

The goal isn't to gouge the customer—they've been through enough. But the model does have to be profitable. While there are some direct cremation businesses out there that aggressively market and sell cremation services and do a very good job of it, pricing their offerings right and providing a high-quality service, there are plenty that are simply entering the market, offering everything at a discount, and unknowingly running themselves into the ground in the process. In the meantime, though, those businesses are souring the consumer perception of what these services actually cost. At some point, we're going to have to address that as well.

---

18 "Death of a U.S. Citizen." U.S. Embassy and Consulates. Accessed April 11, 2019. https://jp.usembassy.gov/u-s-citizen-services/death-of-a-u-s-citizen/.

In addition, as cremation rates rise, funeral businesses are going to have to consolidate. Cremation is profitable; however, it is a low-dollar service. That means you need to do a lot more of it to do well. While funeral businesses in small towns may band together to streamline resources and increase productivity, there will likely be more merging or sales to the acquisition companies out there. But the changes aren't only limited to the method of disposal.

Nothing Is Exempt from Disruption—Not Even Death

Technology will also play a huge part in those changing consumer preferences. Virtually every sector of the economy has received a disruptive technological model, and it's just a matter of time for us. We've already discussed the impact of ride-sharing apps and the fact that Amazon has changed the way millions of people around the world shop for almost every product imaginable—urns included. What's to prevent the same kind of disruption from occurring in the funeral business?

Some changes are definitely on the way on this front already. For one, the Federal Trade Commission's Funeral Rule, which governs how funeral homes convey their pricing to a customer, is up for review in 2019. Currently, the Funeral Rule dictates that funeral businesses must provide prices to those who ask over the phone and in person. Nonprofit groups like the Consumer Federation of America and the Funeral Consumers Alliance are campaigning for a change, insisting that prices must be posted online for transparency's sake and that not doing so takes advantage of those who are grieving.[19]

---

19 Ann Carrns, "With Funeral Home Rules Due for an Update, There's a Push for Online Prices." *New York Times*. March 2019. https://www.nytimes.com/2019/03/29/your-money/funeral-homes-pricing.html.

Meanwhile, a 2018 study by Funeral Consumers Alliance found that out of the two hundred funeral homes they reviewed, only 16 percent had websites with full price lists online. If the rule changes, our approach to posting prices will have to as well.[20] And it may not just be a change to the Funeral Rule that makes online pricing a necessity. There are currently sites out there like Funeralocity.com that provide pricing in different markets, rewarding those who provide prices online with an "excellence" status.[21] To compete, we may have to meet this consumer-driven standard.

Of course, it's about more than just price. If one funeral business is offering a package that includes cremation and a memorial service for $1,500 and another is providing the same package for $3,500, chances are $2,000 is not the only difference between the two options. While the first may operate out of a strip mall and provide a single funeral director who may be overworked and undertrained, the second may be located in a pristine yet easy-to-find location and assign two or three funeral directors to the memorial service, along with an administrative staff to manage the permitting and documentation. It may unfortunately take a poor-quality service experience for a family to realize that they will indeed get what they pay for, but the difference will eventually reveal itself. And whether or not it seems like it, price isn't a primary motivator in our business.

Of the tens of thousands of surveys Johnson Consulting gets back every year, the three primary reasons people report choosing a particular funeral business are the convenience of the location, the fact that funerals were prewritten, and that the customer has used that business before. They're not mentioning price.

---

20   Carrns, "With Funeral Home Rules Due for an Update, There's a Push for Online Prices."

21   Carrns, "With Funeral Home Rules Due for an Update, There's a Push for Online Prices."

That's the uniqueness of funeral and cemetery services, a factor that those from the outside world don't quite understand. Death is such a personal thing, and when a family has a great experience, they can't imagine how they would ever do it online without going to see Shawn Murphy at Whitney & Murphy Funeral Home in Phoenix, for instance, because he's excellent at what he does and he takes care of everything. It's a much different experience trying to navigate it all online after a parent has just passed away.

Those who haven't been through it before don't necessarily understand the value of that kind of support. And someone will almost definitely create an online solution that makes it simple and easy for first-timers. But there's also no going back—once it's done, you can't undo it. People who do go online once might not do it the same way the second time around. Consumers are bound to realize the loss associated with commoditizing a human life.

As such, I think there will always be a need for funeral and cemetery professionals, even in the distant future. Technology will have its place. It may play a greater role in improving the selection process, for example. Just like we've seen in other industries, online reviews will become increasingly important to help families differentiate between one funeral or cemetery business and another. This is something to keep in mind, especially as you develop a marketing plan.

Tech may also be the solution for those who didn't have a close relationship with the person who passed and just want to get it done. But in many ways, we fix a very particular problem. And part of the solution we provide is basic humanity during one of the most difficult moments a family has to face. We will have to adapt to technology, but, in the end, it probably won't eradicate the human component of the profession. And that means the quality of our employees will continue to matter.

Where to Find Help

We've discussed the reality that as information becomes even more accessible, showing our kids options they've never been privy to before, finding good help will become increasingly challenging. This is another area where you may have to do some advocating, especially if your state requires that funeral professionals be licensed. It can be said that those laws prevent highly qualified professionals from joining your ranks and will only hurt your business in the long run.

When I was working as a funeral arranger, the only experience I had was in accounting, finance, and management. But I had some of the highest customer satisfaction ratings within the organization. Why? Because I knew how to talk to people. I didn't embalm, of course. I didn't have the skills or the interest. But I also knew that learning how to embalm wasn't going to make me a better funeral arranger. That's something states need to realize as well, and it may take some prodding from those of us in the profession. While regulation is certainly important, we need to recognize the areas where we are hindering our own progress.

In April of 2019, Arizona became the first state in the US to recognize out-of-state licenses.[22] It's just one way to make it easier for qualified professionals to practice without all the red tape in our business and beyond. I would think that other states would do well to follow suit. And by banding together with local professional organizations and advocating for change, we can help them get there.

---

22 Eric Boehm, "Arizona Will Be First State to Recognize Out-of-State Occupational Licenses." Reason.com. April 2019. https://reason.com/2019/04/05/arizona-will-be-first-state-to-recognize/.

Don't Forget That Failure Isn't Death

As we think about the present and future of our business, there's another thing that's important to remember: it's okay to make mistakes. We want to provide families with the best possible service, of course, but that doesn't mean you can't try new things. In fact, in order to stay in touch with today's customer, you have to.

You may remember the little experiment I shared earlier: holding a barbecue at my Sun City funeral home and bringing the advertising demographic down to thirty years old on Facebook. While we got a decent turnout, I also received my fair share of disparaging and bizarre comments. People wondered why anyone would ever do such a thing, and they weren't shy about telling me. But I can't let a few people's opinions limit my willingness to try new things. There were plenty of people who came through my doors, grateful for a chance to see what my business was all about and get comfortable with the idea of what their inevitable last hurrah could look like. Those who were horrified probably weren't the kind of customers I'd want anyway. And, of course, if the event hadn't worked at all, there was nothing that would force me to do it again.

Risk doesn't have to be reckless. It can be calculated. And it's the only way to take advantage of the opportunities that the changes today and tomorrow present.

My dad likes to say that you can either make things happen or wonder what happened. I don't know about you, but I'd prefer to be in the former category. Risk doesn't have to be reckless. It can be calculated. And it's the only way to take advantage of the opportunities that the changes today and tomorrow present. It has been said that is okay to fail—that is how we learn—but even better is to fail fast and then adjust!

There are scary aspects in every part of life. You have to look at your worst fears and think about whether there's something you can do about them. If you're worried that Amazon will infiltrate our space and provide full-fledged funeral services online, it's time to start teaming up with other businesses in your area or figure out how you can offer a similar set of options yourself.

It may not seem like it, but this business has always been changing—from the time it originated with the help of ambulance drivers and carpenters, to the evolution of acquisition firms, to the rise in technology firms in our space. Change is fun. It can be exciting—especially if you're on the front lines. And, like death and taxes, it is inevitable.

Luckily, though, things don't move too quickly in this business. Mark Twain once stated, "When the end of the world comes, I want to be in Cincinnati, because it's always twenty years behind the times." The funeral business is the proverbial Cincinnati here. You've got time before they close the book on your story—and ample opportunity to make it into everything you want it to be.

I hope something in this book has sparked an aha moment for you—one or more ways that you can build the kind of business and future you want. In the end, your success is only limited by your vision. The great beyond can be as great as you make it. Don't be afraid to think big and dig deep.

Conclusion

Throughout this book, we've talked about the many factors that make the funeral and cemetery profession unique. But this business is also just like any other part of life—especially when it comes to growth and progress. Take my golf swing, for example. When I started playing, I went out and tried to learn on my own. I read what I could in books and online, asked my dad to teach me what he knew, and made a slew of mistakes that gradually made me a better player. But at some point, I stopped progressing. I just couldn't improve any further. Frustrated and stuck, I finally reached out to a professional trainer who specialized in improving swings.

"Well," he told me, "your issue has a cause and a symptom. Addressing the symptom is a quicker process, but it won't necessarily get you as far as you can go. Fixing the cause is much slower. You may have to take two steps back to go one step forward. But in the end, you'll be a better golfer. Do you want to address the cause or the symptom?"

I picked the cause. It took some work—a step-by-step breakdown that felt tedious at times—but I was able to create a more consistent outcome for my game. Now, I consider myself an eleven handicapper, though others might call me a sandbagger. But at the end of the day, I play golf much more consistently and better because I learned how to do it right from a pro.

The same goes for getting business assistance—whether it's from an accountant, a coach, or someone else who can provide specialized support. In almost every case, it can't help but make you better.

There are a number of reasons people avoid specialists. Sometimes, they believe they can just do it themselves. Other times, they don't want to invest the time and money to get what they need. But there is nothing that could be more exemplary of penny wise and pound foolish than doing that. I've never been afraid to spend a little cash if it has the potential to make me more efficient. Why? I know the worst thing that can happen is that I might realize it wasn't the right decision and move on. But I never want to look back and say, "I wish I would have tried that."

It's amazing how easy it is to put yourself in that regretful position, though. It can be scary to take a new path and invest in the resources necessary to make you more successful. But you have to remember that there is nothing wrong with taking a couple of steps back if it will get you further along at some point down the line. For me, it comes down to staying organized, handling the tasks I'm qualified to take care of, and putting trust in others to manage the areas that don't fall within my skill set. I don't always do a perfect job, but most of the time, I make the kinds of decisions that benefit me and my companies in the long run.

The older I get, the more I realize life is short—especially in this profession. Hopefully, with this book in hand, you'll be able to learn at a much quicker pace than I ever did. And once you've put the relevant suggestions and strategies found here into place, you may find that as you look to start, improve, or sell your business, the experience and support of Johnson Consulting also fits into the equation for your success.

In our profession, even the large businesses—those operating with $1,750,000 in revenue and no more than five to ten employees—are actually small by most industries' standards. They typically don't have nearly enough knowledge, resources, and skills to navigate and grow their businesses successfully. That's why getting outside support from someone who can offer a broader perspective is so vital.

The funeral and cemetery businesses are all I've ever been in—particularly the financial side. I started out in operations and eventually took on the numbers. I decided to get boots-on-the-ground experience to see how it all worked *after* building expertise on the books. That makes the way I've modeled Johnson Consulting a very valuable asset to those seeking insight on the financial aspect of their organizations.

My team and I have built a company with experience that is second to none in our business. We're not funeral and cemetery service operators who are trying to figure out how to spread information on our personal success in a single market; we're established professionals who are experienced in managing multiple funeral, cemetery, and cremation operations across North America as if they were our own (and in some instances they were!). Rather than offering advice based on the lens of one particular business, we can provide the unique perspective that comes from working with hundreds of operations at one time or collaborating with companies that have billion-dollar market caps. That differs from virtually every private funeral or cemetery business owner and consultant out there. And it's why any funeral or cemetery operation—no matter where they are and how much success they have had—can benefit from picking our brains.

I've heard countless private owners say that corporate-owned firms don't serve their customers well. I don't believe this is always the case, as there are private funeral organizations that are just as guilty. But one thing they can't argue with is the quality of corporate businesses' approach in ensuring the financial operations are on target, that there is a strong strategic plan in place, and that the operations are working toward a particular vision. Johnson Consulting brings that kind of knowledge and process strategy to the table, along with a strong awareness of the care and attention that go into running a private operation. We love this profession, and we remain dedicated to giving back, donating close to a million dollars to associations in our field.

We also give free advice—it's your choice whether you'd like to engage further after speaking to our team (a list of the services we offer follows the conclusion). But whether it's saving you money on a purchase, maximizing the value you get on a sale, or streamlining your own systems to boost productivity, our services pay for themselves, often many times over.

We've now reached our end. As you navigate the next life for your business, it can be overwhelming to think about the changes that are coming your way as well as how to make your mark in this profession—and on the many families who depend on you for support. But determining your next steps doesn't have to be a grave affair. Death will always be around, and that means people will always need us. What those needs look like may shift, but if you can meet them, you won't only stay alive in this profession; you'll thrive.

You don't have to do it alone, though. Whether the next call you make is to us at Johnson Consulting, your local business association, or a trusted mentor, don't hesitate to seek out the people that can help you navigate the new terrain. After all, so much of life is about who you spend it with—and it pays to choose well.

Finally, as the sun sets on our time together, you have my best wishes for success. No matter what the future holds, I'll see you on the other side.

Our Services

Here are some of the options Johnson Consulting offers:

JCG Succession Services

- **Selling Your Businesses**: It never ceases to amaze me that owners make the decision to sell their businesses without any assistance. Almost everyone hires a real estate agent for help selling their homes. They realize that because it's not something they do on a regular basis, it's certainly worth their while to get professional assistance. Why wouldn't you apply the same logic to your business? After all it's your most valuable asset, and you only get one chance to sell it. As such, the goal should be to not only maximize the value and bring in as much cash as you can but also to maintain the reputation you've built—which will be associated with the name on the sign for the foreseeable future. In the end, you'll find that JCG will get you higher than the highest value, which results in us paying for ourselves.

  During the processes, there is so much to think about, much of which owners aren't aware. Due diligence, determining when to introduce your staff to the new owner, and working with an attorney who can support the process (unfortunately, attorneys are notorious for taking down deals in our business because they don't understand it) are all crucial tasks that fall under the umbrella of sales. Johnson Consulting can help with making the right decisions on all of these elements.

- **Acquisition Assistance**: Johnson Consulting helps people buy businesses by taking them through the process of collecting the data and formulating the structures necessary to make the most prudent decisions. After all, once you overpay, you can't go back. That makes us a critical resource for those considering adding another operation to their portfolio.
- **Business Valuations**: To figure out where you want to go, you need to know exactly where you are, which means identifying your enterprise value. Johnson Consulting provides both limited and detailed business valuations, which can be used to identify the right time to sell, create a strong succession plan, and determine how much you can afford in new debt if you're considering a loan.

Accounting and Financial Management

- **Monthly Financial Statements**: Good record keeping and accounting is essential to maintaining a healthy business. It provides you with a pulse on your business, no matter what stage it's at. It also allows for growth and troubleshooting and ensures that, when it is time to sell or pass your operation down to the next generation, your house is not just in working order but tip-top shape. It also takes a fair bit of time, and if you're the owner, that's not how you should be spending those precious hours. With our web-based applications, owners can focus their attention on what really matters to them, and rest assured that everything else is under control. In addition, our industry benchmarks serve as a huge "ah-ha" moment for owners, providing data they would never have access to which helps them make powerful decisions about the present and future of their businesses.

- **Loan Sourcing**: In an industry marked by so much goodwill, it's not always easy to find a loan. Whether you're looking to buy a business yourself or sell your existing operation to your son, daughter, or an employee, Johnson Consulting can help you navigate the process and connect you to those willing to provide the financing you need.

Funeral and Cemetery Business Coaching and Consulting

- **Coaching and Consulting**: Getting outside perspective is priceless, especially for owners and senior management teams. It's a simple way to ensure that you're seeing the forest for the trees. It is invaluable in helping to keep leaders on task when it comes to a business's bigger picture—especially in the current climate, with so many changes coming down the pipeline. I challenge those who have never worked with a professional coach before to try it, just for a year, and see what they get out of it.

- **Incentive-Based Compensation Plans**: The right kind of incentive-based compensation plan can be an incredible motivator, driving staff to provide the very best customer service and boosting bottom lines in the process. The wrong kind can be devastating to a business and require significant time and energy to boot. Johnson Consulting helps businesses build the best program for their business and reap the corresponding benefits.

- **Performance Analysis**: If you know you need to make a change but you're not sure where to start, getting a thorough performance analysis is a terrific first step. Johnson Consulting looks at each area of the four-legged stool—workplace, marketplace, customer service, and financial management—to provide a 360-degree assessment of what's happening within an organization.

- **Strategic Planning**: A good strategic plan is essential to continued success, but you can't emcee your own. At Johnson Consulting, we're expert strategic planners, but I bring in an outside consultant to conduct them for our company, because it's necessary to be able to sit down and offer my thoughts as well. As such, getting an outside firm to come in and run things for you goes a long way.

JCG Performance Tracker

- **Customer Survey and Sales Analysis**: JCG Performance Tracker (JCGPerformanceTracker.com) is the complete customer experience management tool that evaluates your staff's performance, streamlines your success plans, and improves your bottom line. Some of the largest funeral businesses in the United States have benefited from this inexpensive but instrumental feature that drives performance with very little involvement as an owner. Performance Tracker also has features for driving online reviews as well as options for texting and a follow-up card program.

  The JCG Performance Tracker™ provides funeral homes and cemeteries with timely, accurate metrics on customer service and sales performance, allowing you to closely monitor arranger, location, and company performance and take actionable measures to improve your business. Visit www.jcgperformancetracker.com to learn more.

An outside company can also help with accountability, holding you to any processes, procedures, or standards you decide to set. They can help you work *on* the business, when it's far easier to get caught up in spinning your wheels working *in* it.

Johnson Consulting Group was created for partnership and designed for business success. For more information and testimonials on how we've helped hundreds of operations like yours, head to http://www.johnsonconsulting.com/.